The Rich
and the Rest of Us

The Rich

and the
REST *of*
US

A POVERTY MANIFESTO

TAVIS SMILEY
CORNEL WEST

SMILEYBOOKS

Distributed by Hay House, Inc.
Carlsbad, California • New York City
London • Sydney • Johannesburg
Vancouver • Hong Kong • New Delhi

Published in the United States by: SmileyBooks, 250 Park Avenue South, Suite #201, New York, NY 10003 • www.SmileyBooks.com

Distributed in the United States by: Hay House, Inc.: www. hayhouse.com • *Published and distributed in Australia by:* Hay House Australia Pty. Ltd.: www.hayhouse.com.au • *Published and distributed in the United Kingdom by:* Hay House UK, Ltd.: www. hayhouse.co.uk • *Published and distributed in the Republic of South Africa by:* Hay House SA (Pty), Ltd.: www.hayhouse.co.za • *Distributed in Canada by:* Raincoast: www.raincoast.com • *Published and distributed in India by:* Hay House Publishers India: www.hayhouse.co.in

Cover design: Juan Roberts/Creative Lunacy
Interior Design: Cindy Shaw/Creative Details.net

Grateful acknowledgment is made for permission to reprint previously published material: John Scalzi, excerpt from "Being Poor." Reprinted with permission. http://whatever.scalzi. com/2005/09/03/being-poor/

Library of Congress Control Number: 2012934043

Tradepaper ISBN: 978-1-4019-4063-8
Digital ISBN: 978-1-4019-4064-5

15 14 13 12   5 4 3 2
1st edition, April 2012
2nd edition, April 2012

Printed in the United States of America

For poor people in America

Contents

Introduction

"If we think we have ours and don't owe any time or money or effort to help those left behind, then we are a part of the problem rather than the solution to the fraying social fabric that threatens all Americans."

—Marian Wright Edelman

Sometimes, we can't help but marvel at this blessed, collaborative journey we're on together. It is rare indeed when a philosopher from the halls of academia and a broadcaster from the public arena can become one voice, one mind, and one heart committed to raising consciousness about—as our mutual hero Dr. Martin Luther King, Jr. so eloquently phrased it—"things that matter."

We have traveled thousands of miles together, conducted countless media interviews together; we've sat in homes, walked through communities, and spoken at town hall meetings together. And now, here we are, collaborating on our first book together on a subject that matters to us deeply.

We are concerned about poverty in America because it has impacted our lives, our outreach, the missions we've embraced, and our roles as democratic thinkers.

For my dear brother, Tavis, poverty is not an abstraction; it was the story of his childhood. He didn't grow up associating poverty with Black ghettos, run-down barrios, or slums. Tavis, the oldest of ten kids, grew up in a Bunker Hill, Indiana, trailer park with mostly poor whites. His working-poor, struggling parents, Emory and Joyce Smiley, and his grandmother (Big Mama) ran a strict Pentecostal household in a space that wasn't built for 13 people. When Tavis's aunt was murdered, the Smiley home became the safety net for her four children. He still recalls the humiliation of going to school in hand-me-down clothes and shoes with cardboard stuffed in them to cover the holes in the soles. His success today did not, perhaps cannot, erase the imprint of poverty from his psyche.

Poverty matters deeply to my abiding friend, philosopher, and Princeton University Professor, Dr. Cornel West. His father, Clifton L. West, Jr., a contractor for the U.S. government; and his mother, Irene B. West, a teacher and later a pioneering school principal, were actively involved in the early Civil Rights Movement. Often, when reflecting on his formative years, Doc tells me he was inspired by the "sincere black militancy of Malcolm X, the defiant rage of the Black Panther Party, and the Black theology of James Cone." As student-body president at John F. Kennedy High School in Sacramento, California, Doc organized protests demanding Black studies courses at his and other local high schools, as well as marched in civil rights demonstrations. Doc has been a champion for racial and social justice since childhood. Grounded in the traditions of the Black Baptist Church and music, Doc has always been concerned about fighting poverty both at home and around the world.

Poverty matters to us because it mattered to Dr. King. Our work and witness are inspired by his words, "I choose to identify with the underprivileged, I choose to identify with the poor, I choose to give my life for the hungry, I choose to give my life for those who have been left out of the sunlight of opportunity." For us, ending poverty is squarely rooted in the legacy of a King who fought against poverty until his dying day on April 4, 1968. Lest we forget that, Dr. King's final trip, his final mission, was to go stand beside the poor sanitation workers in Memphis who were fighting for better wages, bargaining rights, and safer working conditions. Dr. King's last battles involved the eradication of poverty.

In 2011, we launched *Smiley & West,* a weekly program from PRI that gave us the opportunity to take some of our private dialogue to public radio. We envisioned a down-to-earth format with "real-people conversations" similar to the ones heard at the local coffee house, cocktail party, barbershop, or beauty salon. To that end, a portion of the show is called, "Take 'Em To Task." It's a segment where listeners call in to turn the tables on us and ask questions or challenge the ideas, issues, and actions we pursue.

Edith was one of those "Take 'Em To Task" callers who challenged our position on poverty. She'd heard us preach about it, complain about it, and challenge politicians and other leaders who we felt either made it worse or weren't doing or saying anything at all about it.

"Well," Edith asked us, "what are you two prepared to do about it?"

It was a question we took to heart. We asked ourselves, "What more can a philosopher and broadcaster do about poverty?" The answer was surprisingly simple. Do what we do best—use our public platforms to raise consciousness and raise the issue of poverty higher on the American agenda.

With our mutual passions stoked, we made the decision to inaugurate "The Poverty Tour: A Call to Conscience," an 18-city bus tour that began on August 6, 2011, designed to highlight the plight of America's poor of all races, colors, and creeds.

Although several major media outlets credited us in 2011 for helping to place poverty on the national agenda, our intent wasn't to be first out of the gate on this issue. Our goal was to put a human face on poverty so that the persistent poor, near poor, and new poor will not be ignored or rendered invisible during this unprecedented wave of economic downturn. At this juncture, it was clear to us that too often people weren't connecting the dots between the new face of American poverty and the extraordinary decades-long increase in wealth inequality in the American economic system. The Great Recession and the avalanche of home foreclosures that followed are only one part of the story. We believe that to do more, you have to know more—more of the truth.

Veterans; former factory, marketing, and construction workers; single mothers; married couples; fathers; and teens were just as anxious to tell their stories as we were to hear them. The reaction to our tour bus ranged from welcoming and grateful to hostile and picketing —and we would have it no other way. One group of protesters in Detroit insisted that the sole motivation of the tour was to bash President Barack Obama.

Admittedly, it would have been nice at that time to hear the President and other prominent leaders in public discourse just *say* the words "poor" or "poverty." Instead, we were getting an overdose of sound-bite politics but unsound public policy on poverty in America. Although many of his Republican critics would like us to believe differently, President Obama didn't create the Great Recession, nor did he create poverty. Even POTUS isn't that omnipotent.

After the tour, we aired Poverty Tour highlights as part of a weeklong special on *Tavis Smiley* on PBS to a very positive reception from viewers, yet we were nagged by the thought that we hadn't explored the complicated layers of poverty deeply enough. These feelings intensified as we listened to certain politicians cruelly and crudely disparage the poor. Beyond sound-bite competitions, these candidates for high office, protected with gilded lives of wealth and privilege, seem to know nothing about poverty or the poor. They claim to be concerned about the middle class, but they must have missed the memo; the new poor are the former middle class.

To continue this important conversation, we decided to bring together some of the best minds in the nation to unpack the conundrum of increasing poverty in the richest nation in the world. This intention gave birth to "Remaking America: From Poverty to Prosperity," the January 12, 2012, symposium held in Washington, DC, at George Washington University. The gathering featured such distinctive thought leaders as Suze Orman, Michael Moore, Barbara Ehrenreich, Majora Carter, Roger A. Clay, Jr., and Vicki B. Escarra; it was broadcast live on C-SPAN.

While ironing out details for the symposium, we were contacted by a major publisher about translating our experiences and observations from the Poverty Tour into a book. Although this wasn't something we had planned, the invitation resonated. We were very disturbed and disappointed by much of the media coverage about poverty. Most seemed to focus on the job loss fueled by the bailout of America's "banksters" and home foreclosures. Such conversations were myopic, giving the impression that our woes will end as soon as the economy bounces back. *Let us be clear: An economic uptick or recovery will not solve what we witnessed while traveling across this country.* Bouncing back won't reconfigure the nation's embedded equation that keeps the rich richer and the poor poorer.

We not only met the faces of poverty on the tour,

we were also exposed to poverty's historic legacy and evolution. Poverty is not the stepchild of the Great Recession; poverty has always been a part of American life. It is a state of being that this country has valiantly faced at times, but, more frequently, recoiled from in fear and condemnation.

The fact that one percent of the nation's richest individuals controls 42 percent of the country's wealth is a stunning revelation in the wake of a recession. But, through the lens of history, we see the institutionalized precedent of greed meticulously entangled in this nation's very fabric. In fact, one could argue that America was a corporation before it was a country.

The Poverty Tour provided the opportunity to meet many people who had been living paycheck to paycheck even before the economic downturn. To so quickly slide from the great middle into the underworld of the poor validated our suspicions that perhaps these citizens never really were bona fide, middle class Americans. Indeed, some economists assert that the middle class evaporated decades ago. Those in jeopardy often maintained their middle class identities by holding fast to the belief that every generation was destined to live lives better than that of their parents and grandparents. Isn't that what the big-screen television in the living room meant?

We met the casualties of this exploded myth.

And we discovered a surprising playing-field equalizer. No matter how successful those who were raised in poverty become, they are haunted by the fear of reliving it. Those who have actually experienced poverty in their lifetimes are better equipped to cope than those who have not. For the first time in decades, the American dream for millions has turned into a nightmare, leaving them shattered and struggling to survive. A nation that now has the blues must learn from a blues people or it may not endure.

What stays with us are memories of a wide-eyed generation suddenly paralyzed by their downsized American Dream. Just a decade ago, Americans were able to satisfy their lust for the celebrity lifestyles of the rich and famous. But, again, poverty isn't a 21st-century phenomenon.

With history as our guide, we can chart the moment Americans got addicted to credit cards and the quest for the American Dream became a shopping mall–like adventure. Spending a cold night camped out in a parking lot to be first in line when a store opens and getting trampled by a crowd competing for "the sale of the day" doesn't even seem to matter. But deep down we knew we'd never attain the lifestyles we saw on television. As brainwashed, robotic consumers armed with unending credit, we sought to transform our living-large fantasies into reality. Now, our supersized ambitions have been downsized.

The "new poor" find themselves standing shoulder to shoulder at the welfare office, food pantry, or thrift store with people they used to disregard. As the politicians they elected predict a doomed "entitlement nation" and boast of shredding the poor's safety nets, the former middle class tries to reconcile these contradictions by clinging to the belief that this is a temporary destination, that somehow "they" are still better than "those people."

How do we get folk to understand that there is no "they," there is no "them"? Too many Americans are falling through gaping holes scissored out of America's safety net. Income inequality is real. There is an institutionalized divide between the wealthy and the poor, so that what we now have are the rich and the rest of us.

We are at a critical turning point in America, and we are obsessed with the ambitious goal of changing how we think about, talk about, and act on the issue of poverty and the poor. This book is an unapologetic affirmation of the rising tide of restlessness the world over. The Occupy Wall Street movement is the most recent example of the tsunami of moral outrage and resistance that has now washed over 82 countries and five continents.

With nearly one in two Americans now living in or near poverty, everyday people of all colors have grown weary of the unmitigated greed of the mega-wealthy minority who have steered the economy, not into a ditch, but over a cliff. The rich and powerful's political emissaries are losing their hypnotic effect on the people lying mangled at the bottom. Because economic injustice in America has been overshadowed by greed, because unequal taxation benefits the rich at the expense of everyone else, because our political system has become so paralyzed and acquiescent to the culture of greed and moral decay—the poor are fighting back.

True democracy focuses on the public interest; it defends the common good and protects its citizens—especially the weak and vulnerable. We maintain that no democracy can survive without the powerful notions of compassion and public service. The level of wealth inequality in this country has gotten so far out of hand, the quantity of compassion so thoroughly diminished, that the very future of American democracy is at stake. And that's not hyperbole.

This book serves as a counterpoint to neo-liberal apologists, conservative right-wing pundits, and corporate media puppets who luxuriate in dismissing, demeaning, or denying the reality of America's poor. The faces of poverty are no longer solely relegated to the easily maligned Black, red, or brown people. Poverty of all colors abounds unchecked in our cities, suburbs, and rural communities with ever-growing shameful numbers of impoverished children joining its ranks. Poverty is no longer confined by class or color; like an unrestrained and deadly virus, it doesn't discriminate.

The Poverty Tour reaffirmed our respect for the dignity and humanity of every American—especially the unemployed and the underemployed. If Dr. King were alive today, he'd still unflinchingly use his prophetic voice to declare a deficiency of will to do what's right by our fellow citizens. Just as he did in life, Dr. King would denounce the poverty of opportunity, poverty of affirmation, poverty of courage, poverty of compassion, and poverty of imagination in our modern times. In the spirit of Dr. King, we wish to enlist your help as we attempt to unsettle, unnerve, and unseat the powers that deny and downplay the rights of poor people in this nation and in the world. We're not Dr. King—or even trying to be—but we do believe that the very future of this democracy is inextricably linked to how seriously we heed his call to care for and concern ourselves with the plight of the poor.

With history and a host of preeminent and everyday voices offering honest testimony and compelling analysis, we make the case for radical social transformation. We try to demonstrate how the elimination of poverty is possible if and when we break from traditional paradigms and map a new course based on shared humanity and shared accountability.

This manifesto, backed by stubborn facts and damning statistics, will erase any doubt that we are just experiencing a crisis in our country; we are dangerously close to cementing a permanent American catastrophe.

We set out on a journey to raise America's consciousness about poverty. Along the way, the fight-back of poor people emboldened us.

This poverty manifesto is our tribute to them.

Tavis Smiley   Cornel West

Los Angeles
April 2012

CHAPTER 1

Portrait of Poverty

*"I'm not the homeless man down on the corner
begging for change. I am anybody
living anywhere U.S.A."*

—Paul, Birmingham, AL

Guilford County, North Carolina, resident Diane
Struble wanted readers of her local newspaper to understand that poverty in America has a new face. In 21st-
century America, the poor are no longer just the permanently unemployable, the recently incarcerated, or the
mentally ill. Disheveled vagrants who push overstuffed,
wobbly wheeled carts down abandoned streets, who
sleep across sidewalk grates, or who stay in overcrowded
shelters are no longer the reigning faces of poverty.

Even after our poverty tour ended, we're still haunted by the tragic and triumphant stories of Americans
grappling with poverty. Diane Struble's story, which

aired on CBS News in late 2011, reinforced our commitment. During the tour we gazed into the eyes and felt the beating hearts of the needy without the distance of a television screen or a Plexiglass shield: We came face to face with poverty. The folk we met were white like Diane; Black like us; brown, yellow, and every other shade. Poverty refused to discriminate on the basis of religious creed or ethnic identity.[1]

While many whom we met fit what some define as the "old poor" (people who were impoverished before the beginning of the "Great Recession" in late 2007), we were also gathered with shockingly large numbers of the "new poor"—citizens who were once bona fide members of America's middle class, whose lives have been ravaged by the new economy's middle class. They are the grandchildren and great grandchildren of a generation that embodied artist Norman Rockwell's *American Dream.* They once possessed relatively predictable and reasonably comfortable lives until they were inexplicably cast into a maelstrom of economic dispossession and spiritual despair. When the bottom fell out of the American Dream, the formerly lower, middle, and upper-middle classes found themselves recast in the nightmares of the downtrodden. Their possessions repossessed, gone; their lifestyles drastically altered; their dignity destroyed; and their identities radically transformed. Many now feel inexplicably cursed by something that was never supposed to happen to "them." They remain sober, indeed somber, faced with the frightening possibility of being destitute in the future and dependent on meager public assistance with no other resources.

Diane Struble's newspaper op-ed painted a painfully realistic portrait of the new poor. She and her husband Todd had both done all the right things. Both were college-educated; they enjoyed a solidly middle class, combined annual income of $85,000. During the CBS News interview, the couple explained how Todd had lost his job as a paralegal in November 2009, and hadn't found steady work since. The Strubles have eight children, four of whom still live at home. They get by on Diane's school teacher salary of $22,000 a year, which is below the poverty line. Diane cashed in her 401(K) plan, and Todd had withdrawn all he could from his pension. At the time of the interview, the couple had about $25 in cash and $100 in the bank. Their 14-year-old son, Ben, recalled how the family ate soup every day for two weeks: "That's kind of rough," he confessed.

"When was the last time you cried?" CBS News reporter Byron Pitts asked Diane. Her face resting on her cupped hands, tears clouding her worried hazel eyes, Diane whispered: "Last night."

"We are the growing edge of poverty," Todd interjected, adding that they represent the "greater and greater divide between the haves and the have-nots."

TO HAVE AND TO HAVE-NOT

While the incomes of the richest 1 percent of Americans—those earning $380,000 or more—have grown by 33 percent over the past 20 years, the income growth for the other 90 percent of Americans, including the middle class, has been at a virtual standstill. Today, an American "in the top 1 percent takes in an average of $1.3 million per year, while the average American earns just $33,000 per year."[2]

Real annual income of poor, middle class & rich

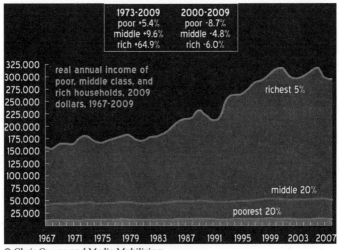

© Chris Caruso and Media Mobilizing
Graphic Design: Nate Adams and Mindi Mumaw

The number of people living in poverty rose by 2.6 million between 2009 and 2010. Revised Census numbers released in 2011 revealed that the number of Americans living in poverty was closer to 50 million. In the Census Bureau's history of tracking poverty statistics, the Great Recession marked the fourth period of consecutive annual increases in 52 years.

POVERTY TIMELINE

Year	Poverty Percent	
1959	22.4 percent	Official tracking of the country's poverty rate begins
1964	19.0 percent	President Lyndon B. Johnson declares "War on Poverty"
1969	13.7 percent	Johnson's Great Society efforts help reduce poverty
1973	11.1 percent	National poverty rate at an almost 20-year low
1979	12.4 percent	Vietnam War, Conservative backlash, poverty ticks up
1983	15.2 percent	A recession from mid-1981 to late 1982 takes its toll on the poor
1989	13.1 percent	Economy steadies, poverty rate drops in Ronald Reagan's 2nd term
1992	14.5 percent	Reagan drastically slashes government benefit programs, poverty rises
1993	15.1 percent	Ten-year gains reversed; Poverty back to 1983 level
1994	14.5 percent	Economy perks, poverty level slightly reduced
1996	13.7 percent	Poverty rate drops, Clinton introduces drastic welfare reform efforts
2000	11.3 percent	Poverty rates fall dramatically due mostly to the opulent 1990s
2007	12.5 percent	Poverty ticks up, 37.3 million in poverty before the recession begins
2008	13.2 percent	Another 2.5 million fall below the poverty line
2009	14.3 percent	6.3 million more in poverty since 2007
2010	15.1 percent	The largest percentage of long-term poor in five decades

Number in Poverty and Poverty Rate: 1959 to 2010

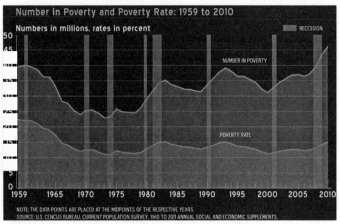

© Chris Caruso and Media Mobilizing
Graphic Design: Nate Adams and Mindi Mumaw

The biggest blows to the already shrinking middle class were record unemployment and a housing bubble that burst, resulting in the foreclosure of nearly 4 million homes. In Don Peck's penetrating investigative piece in *The Atlantic,* "Can the Middle Class Be Saved?" he explained how the housing boom helped hollow out the middle class by allowing "working-class and middle class families to raise their standard of living despite income stagnation or downward job mobility."[3]

The number of Americans who had been unemployed for six months or more in 2009 reached 6.3 million—the largest number since 1948, when the government began counting the long-term unemployed. For the first time in decades, the percentage of working families in poverty rose to 31.2 percent, or 10.2 million people.

We met plenty of skilled people searching for jobs as we traveled from city to city. At Prairie Opportunity, Inc., a Mississippi nonprofit that offers aid and services to the needy, we met folk like Alicia Brooks, a single woman with computer training who had been unemployed for about six months and, at the time, received no income. In Clarksdale, Mississippi, we visited Coahoma Opportunities, Inc., another community service organization, where directors shared heart-breaking stories of clients like Arric Ford, 39, a single father living with his children, ages 13 and 16. Ford, who had been unemployed since March 2011, had been denied unemployment benefits. With no income, he swallowed his pride and turned to Coahoma for help.

During our visit with the University of Wisconsin's Odyssey Project in Madison, Wisconsin, we met former Chicago resident Kegan Carter. Tall and personable, she graciously invited us to her house for a home-cooked meal. Because of the size of our crew, we declined but were blessed to hear her story. Carter was homeless the first six months after arriving in Madison—pregnant and desperately looking for a new start. While visiting the public library, she happened to notice a flyer for the Odyssey Project—a program that helps low-income adults achieve higher education. She credits the agency for changing her life. It is the reason the single mother of three has earned a degree from the University of Wisconsin in English and plans to go to graduate school.

At the time of our visit, Carter was getting by, making a few bucks designing the project's newsletter. In a country struggling to find its footing in the competitive, globalized marketplace, prosperous futures for Americans like Carter and others—the unskilled, low-skilled, or even highly skilled—are highly questionable. Manufacturing jobs being outsourced overseas, weakened labor unions, corporations that place profit over working people, and a rapidly growing divide between the rich and the poor have virtually eliminated the middle class: An unprepared America struggles with the specter of an American Dream that is morphing into a distinctively American nightmare.

20TH-CENTURY POVERTY VERSUS 21ST-CENTURY POVERTY

Christopher Jenks, who grew up in a white, middle class family in Minneapolis-St. Paul, had become homeless after his successful career in sales and marketing came to a crashing halt. On the Poverty Tour, we had become fans of the Marguerite Casey Foundation's *Equal Voice Newspaper*—an extraordinary online publication dedicated to sharing stories about families living in poverty from multiple perspectives. *Equal Voice* allowed us to discover Jenks's plight.

Stubbornly prideful, Jenks refused to apply for public aid while he feverishly sought work. During the hard times, he panhandled on a freeway exit ramp and lived in his car. With no prospects in sight, Jenks finally gave in and applied for government help. Never in his wildest dreams had he imagined himself homeless and surviving on food stamps.

"It's either that or I die," Jenks said, "I want a job. So

do a lot of other Americans that have been caught up in this tragedy."

Like Jenks, millions of middle class Americans find themselves caught up in an economic "tragedy" they never imagined could happen to them. Most people living from paycheck to paycheck could probably imagine hard times if they ever lost their jobs; but the middle class's instant slide into poverty didn't seem possible, not in America. In a country where hard work, grit, and education have always been touted as the pathway to prosperity and the "American Dream," living in genuine poverty never entered into most middle class minds.

During the 2012 Republican presidential primary contests, candidates spoke of the poor as if their constituents didn't include the millions who now fall under the categories of "poor" or "near poor." Food stamp recipients became the poster children of big government gone awry. Several GOP candidates spoke of overhauling welfare programs, but former House Speaker Newt Gingrich invoked the familiar specter of negative racial stereotypes when he labeled President Barack Obama the "best food stamp President in American history" and called on African Americans in particular to "demand paychecks and not be satisfied with food stamps."

Ronnie McHugh, of Spring City, Pennsylvania, who happens to be white, was so angered by Gingrich's comment and the audience's applause to it that she turned off her TV. At the time, McHugh—a divorcée with no savings and living off an $810 Social Security check every month—wasn't feeling Gingrich's charged rhetoric.

"I'd give a million dollars if I could find a job. I'm 64

years old, and no one wants to hire me," said McHugh.

The debate audience should walk in her shoes, McHugh told a reporter from *Equal Voice.* If so, perhaps they'd appreciate government programs—*any* program—that helped hard-working people impacted by the recession.

"I would tell them I had a husband who made $150,000 a year; I had a good salary. We were both laid off at the same time by the same company, and I've never been able to rally from that," McHugh said.[4]

Situations like hers were addressed during the January 2012 symposium, "Remaking America: From Poverty to Prosperity," hosted by Tavis and broadcast live on C-SPAN. Barbara Ehrenreich, best-selling author of more than a dozen books, including *Nickel and Dimed* and *Bait and Switch*, spoke to present-day attitudes regarding the poor:

> "The theory for a long time—coming not only from the right but also from some Democrats—is that poverty means that there's something wrong with your character, that you've got bad habits, you've got a bad lifestyle, you've made the wrong choices.
>
> "I would like to present an alternative theory . . . poverty is a shortage of money. And the biggest reason for that shortage of money is that most working people are not paid enough for their work and then we don't have work."

Ehrenreich's observations hits the chord of common sense and speaks to poverty in our times. Unfortunately, politicians and most Americans haven't made that transition. We react and respond to the poor as if they're afflicted with some flesh-eating virus and are highly contagious. We deny poverty because we are afraid—afraid that saying the word somehow puts us at risk. We deny poverty because our definitions of it are stuck within a history of bygone eras. This collective psychological black hole of fear threatens so deeply that it often results in moral failure and stalls our efforts to effectively address a potential national pandemic. It paralyzes us and prevents us from courageously facing the facts and coming up with real solutions to help America's "old" and "new" poor.

This brings us back to Guilford County's Diane Struble. Her letter to the local newspaper, based on her family's experience, was an attempt to give voice to the voiceless. In making the distinction between herself and the typical street beggar, Struble was essentially saying that 21st-century poverty is not the 20th-century poverty of our parents' or grandparents' generation.[5]

"THE POOR HOUSE"

There was no official Census taking in America before 1939 when the government started collecting income status information. Consequently, reliable definitions of poverty didn't exist until the 1960s. Yet even without certified figures, there are several sources, primarily social-reform and charitable agencies, that detail the extent of poverty in America from the 18th to the 20th centuries.

In 1969, researcher William B. Hartley used old Bureau of Labor Statistics, manufacturing records, and other sources to estimate that poverty among wage earners in 1870 was around 62 percent. It dropped to 39 percent in 1900 and rose to 44 percent by 1909.

Before social researchers and women's organizations in the early 1900s challenged staid perceptions of poverty or "pauperism" in America, poverty was widely blamed on personal flaws such as immorality, alcoholism, and criminal behavior.[6] A February 17, 1854, *New York Times* article depicted the poor as dishonest and criminal and gave no sympathy to their children: *"There are ten thousand children in this City alone, who are either without parents or friends, or are trained systematically by their parents to vagrancy, beggary, and crime: not only shut out utterly and hopelessly from all moral influences, but exposed day and night to the contamination of crime . . ."*

During the 19th century, the poor held the same status as prostitutes, thieves, and the criminally insane. Long before the welfare system or the Social Security Administration were established, anyone deemed poor or unable to support themselves were sent to the poorhouse. Modeled after the European system, America's poorhouses were shelters of horror. The elderly, widows, and their children were housed with society's outcasts and suffered all sorts of physical neglect and sexual abuse. Local governments provided sparse funding, so residents of all sexes and ages were required to work for their keep, performing tasks that included farming, cooking, laundering, and whatever else was necessary to keep the institutions functioning.

Poorhouses gradually disappeared by the early 20th century as the government established more institutionalized and, arguably, civilized ways to care for the elderly, the sick, the mentally ill, and poor women and children. Nevertheless, the stigma of poverty remained attached to the less fortunate and is still aggressively applied in modern times. Researchers Michael B. Katz and Mark J. Stern, who wrote "Poverty in Twentieth-Century America," provide an extensive history of poverty in America.[7]

They introduce social reformer Robert Hunter's 1904 study, *Poverty,* that "estimated that half the population of New York City lived in absolute poverty—a number that seems neither an exaggeration nor unrepresentative of other large cities."[8] In the early 1900s, "new immigrants and African-Americans" disproportionately represented the masses of "the poor." Still, because of "intermittent participation in the workforce," Katz and Stern noted that about four out of every ten American workers earned poverty wages. Income inequality and poverty worsened between 1896 and 1914 due to cost-of-living increases and declines in the wages of the working poor. Malnourishment and diseases were common. The "real story of widespread, grinding rural poverty," Katz and Stern noted, "began in the 1920s and continued through the Great Depression."[9]

Between the years 1900 and 1920, public opinion about the poor began an incremental shift. This change can be attributed in large part to the Settlement House Movement and bold activism of educated women such as Jane Addams, Lillian Wald, Florence Kelley, Ida B.

Wells-Barnett, Julia Lathrop, and other founders and directors of settlement houses for the poor.

American settlement houses—private nonprofit agencies—were primarily established in poor immigrant neighborhoods and were modeled after Toynbee Hall in London, England. Inspired by religious convictions and a sense of moral obligation, the agencies were much more than institutions for the destitute. Settlement house leaders became vocal and visible advocates for social-welfare reform, arguing that poverty was not necessarily a character flaw but rather a state of being agitated by multiple factors—slave wages, disease, and the death of a spouse. Advocates challenged newspapers' attacks on the poor and took on Industrial Age barons accused of exploiting women and children in sweat shops, factories, and mines. In a sense, settlements houses were early America's think tanks, where recruiting, training, researching, and policy-setting were incorporated into everyday activities. By 1910, about 400 settlement houses were operating in the United States.

Eleanor Roosevelt, the wife of President Franklin D. Roosevelt, was professionally trained in the settlement houses of New York. Her passion and influence had much to do with FDR's social-reform proposals.

Of course, nothing helped improve the image of poverty like the Stock Market Crash of 1929, which led to the Great Depression. Walking in the shoes of poor folk helped the working class sympathize with those whom they once despised. Like the recession today, during the Depression, working-class folk soon discovered how quickly they, too, could become poor. The social reformers' often ignored assertions—that systemic and institutional factors contributed to poverty—were finally deemed valid during the Depression era.

Not only were their claims validated, but much of the research, theories, policies, and practices of social reformers and settlement house leaders were incorporated into FDR's projects and policies, such as his public works programs and Social Security.

POST-WAR POVERTY

Wartime prosperity, rising wages, growth in manufacturing and productivity, declining unemployment, and the expansion of public benefits, all combined, helped to significantly reduce poverty in America in the years after the Depression.

The increased demand for manufacturing products contributed to the transformation of attitudes and roles toward women in the workplace. At the start of World War II, with men by the hundreds of thousands joining the war effort and large and lucrative war contracts waiting to be filled, the United States faced a drastic labor shortage. This void led to the creation of the fictional character "Rosie the Riveter," a caricature that became part of the propaganda campaign created to entice women out of their homes and into factories, shipyards, and war plants. When the United States entered the war, 12 million women (one-quarter of the workforce) were already working, according to the National Park Service's exhibit, "Rosie the Riveter: Women Working During World War II." But, by the end of the war, the number was up to 18 million (one-third of the workforce). All told, between the years 1940 and 1945, female workers in defense industries grew by 462 percent.[10]

After the war, sexism was re-entrenched in the workplace. Women were either laid off or found themselves (once again) relegated to low-paying jobs. Men basically resumed their dominant positions in the workforce. It wasn't until 1964 and the passage of Title VII of the Civil Rights Act, which prohibited discrimination on the basis of race, color, religion, sex, or national origin, that women gained the opportunity to exert themselves somewhat equally into the workforce.

We should note the dramatic drop in poverty between the years 1939 and 1959. Census data collected after 1939 showed that by the end of the Great Depression, 40 percent of all working households under the age of 65 earned poverty wages, which were about $900 per year for a family of four. Katz and Stern described a turnaround by 1959, where 60 percent of American householders earned enough money to lift their families out of poverty.[11]

The dramatic drop in poverty in that 20-year span, however, wasn't reflected in Black and Hispanic households. Although many Blacks who migrated north after World War II found labor and domestic work, thereby earning more money, the poverty rate in 1939 was still a whopping 71 percent for African Americans and 59 percent for America's Latino population.[12]

The 1950s were somewhat prosperous times for the nation, but that decade also marked the beginning of great changes in the American family structure. Households headed by women doubled from 16 percent to 32 percent between 1950 and 1990, but only four out of every ten women who headed households earned more than poverty wages.

The greatest shift in public and political attitudes toward poverty came during the turbulent 1960s in the midst of the Civil Rights Movement. Michael Harrington's classic *The Other America* (1962) forced many Americans to grapple with the conundrum that a country celebrated for its opulence had such glaring income disparities.[13] Harrington's landmark study of poverty in America has been credited as the motivation behind President Johnson's Great Society policies. Although it was President John F. Kennedy who first came in possession of the book, it was Johnson who used it as a guide for his self-proclaimed "War on Poverty" after Kennedy's assassination. Harrington's book was so influential that the *Boston Globe* and other newspapers wrote that Medicaid, Medicare, food stamps, and the expanded Social Security benefits were all traceable to *The Other America*.[14]

The number of families who earned enough to rise out of poverty peaked at 68 percent in 1969. According to Katz and Stern, it dipped again in the 1970s and '80s and, tragically, by 1989, poverty rates in America were back at 1940-era levels.

Due to the rising cost of living, it became harder for one-salary families to stay above the poverty level. In the late 20th century, it was the increased proportion of married women in the workforce and two-income families that helped keep most American families above the poverty line. On the other end of the spectrum, the poverty rate between male- and female-headed households widened. According to the Katz and Stern report, by 1990, the poverty rate for women in male-headed households was 14 percent while households headed by females stood at the higher rate of 17 percent.[15]

By the late 1970s, the face of poverty had reverted to 19th-century levels, and the poor were once again blamed for their circumstances. Since then, poverty has become a political football used to accent government failures and ridicule socio-economic outcomes. Also, by focusing on the disproportionate numbers of Blacks and Latinos who live beneath the poverty line, deceitful messengers successfully re-attached the stigma of personal and social irresponsibility to the images of the impoverished.

Over the decades, Americans have become increasingly aware of severe poverty in Third World countries. Starting in the 1970s, televised images have helped Americans distance themselves from the possibility of ever fitting the definition of "poor." Late-night television commercials present heart-wrenching images of foreign children surrounded by flies, living in villages with no sewers or running water. These depictions of people without sustenance betray the American Dream—the ingrained guarantee of opportunities and success through dogged pursuit of personal wealth. In a nation where instant credit bamboozles consumers, the middle class continues to live in a make-believe bubble of security, forestalling the inevitable based on an elusive promise.

A DREAM DETERRED?

*"It's called the American Dream
because you have to be asleep to believe it."*
—George Carlin

"Between the two of us, my wife and I were making more than $100 grand a year. We lived the middle class highlife of the twos—two salaries, two kids, a two-car garage attached to a four-bedroom house in a nice, quiet neighborhood. Man, we were living the American Dream, but I'm still stunned at how quickly everything changed."

"Samuel" didn't want us to use his real name because, he said, he's well-known in his community—as a Website designer, content provider, and writer. However, he insisted we share his "riches to rags" story.

Both he and his wife are college-educated and had easily found good jobs throughout their careers. In 2009, Samuel lost the full-time job he'd had for six years due to downsizing. But the self-proclaimed "hustler" had already established his own creative-services company. Business was booming—for about six months—until his client base suddenly dried up.

"Major accounts just disappeared. My clients were struggling through the Great Recession like everyone else," Samuel said. "The phones stopped ringing. No one could afford my services. Bills started piling up quickly. Our annual income was cut in half that first year and by a third in 2010."

Although he and his wife made decent money, Samuel explained, they still lived "paycheck to paycheck" and had quickly depleted their savings.

Over 50 job queries went unanswered. The couple could no longer afford private-school tuition and had no choice but to place their children in a "substandard" public school, Samuel said. By the end of 2010, cars had been repossessed; the house was in foreclosure; and he found himself in court "a lot" mostly dealing with back taxes and credit card debt. Family tension was high. The economic ruin culminated with the dissolution of his 15-year marriage. At the age of 50, Samuel, a devastated divorcé, says he finds himself reliving the impoverished days of his early adult life:

> "Every day, a bill collector will call and remind me that my lack of money means I'm now a 'loser' or a 'deadbeat.' I live the life of a coward—afraid to answer my own door out of fear that a bill collector or someone who's come to shut off one of my utilities will be standing there. It's hard to see myself as a contributing member of society or as a good provider now. My pride, my sense of manhood has been nearly destroyed, man."

It wasn't supposed to be this way. The presumed scenario is that you follow all the rules. Everybody knows you can't be successful in these modern times without a college education. So you enroll in college, perhaps you attend a land-grant state college or a prestigious private university. Perhaps you graduated with honors. Debt might have been pouring out of your ears, but still, you make it. With expectations of a fantastic job that matches your fantastic skills, you'll handle the debt—later.

Then, reality hits; you can't find a job in this Recession Economy or the one you secured has been snatched away. You hit the streets, search the want ads and the Internet and newspapers, and social-media sites—nothing.

All seems hopeless. Your life is consumed with massive debt, color-coded bills, and constant calls from malicious debt collectors. You start to lose the symbols of solvency—the car, the house, the financial freedom, and the life you were promised if you played by the rules.

Welcome to the ranks of the poor.

What happened to the American Dream—the one we've heard about since kindergarten, the one we've read about and were indoctrinated to believe in—the ever-so-plausible happy ending that could be secured with nothing more than a little sweat and dogged determination?

We could, as did comedian George Carlin, cynically dismiss the dream as a myth created by the highfaluting founders of this country. But that would be facile and untrue. Our belief is in the validity of Martin Luther King's dream, which is a dialectical critique of the American Dream. King's dream affirmed the humanity of those overlooked and left out by those in power. So, his dream was deeply rooted in the American Dream but placed a premium on poor people. That said, the American Dream is our nation's brand. It is the strategic marketing plan that has lured millions of immigrants to these shores with hopes of accomplishing wonders unimaginable in their native lands. It is the symbol of our historic rise to a world power in less than 200 years. Yet, the "dream" is not the real problem. America's denial is. Just as we still adhere to an outdated conception of poverty, we have brought ourselves and our society to the brink by our refusal to draft a new dream for our times. If we don our historical lens, we'll see a once-democratic vision now compromised and corrupted by materialism and greed that has morphed into an insatiable, capitalist monster that threatens our very existence.

This was the dream of 17th-century Puritans who fled religious persecution in England seeking freedom and opportunities in the "New World." Yet "life, liberty, and the pursuit of happiness" as "unalienable rights" bestowed by God in the Declaration of Independence seems at odds with America's original sins—genocide against Amerindians and enslavement of Africans.

The dream of equality, hope, and liberty was woven deeply into the fabric of America. The Statue of Liberty gifted to the United States and erected in 1886 personified the country's ideal values—despite the legal exclusion of Chinese that same year. Millions of New York–bound immigrants were welcomed with these generous words inscribed at Lady Liberty's feet: "Give me your tired, your poor/Your huddled masses yearning to breathe free."

Ironically, it wasn't until 1931, when historian James Truslow Adams penned the "American Dream" in *The Epic of America* that the phrase became popular enough to become the nation's mantra.[16]

As America became more prosperous and powerful, the visionary goals of comforting the poor were drowned out by the bombastic drumbeat for war and the seemingly irresistible cadence of the pursuit of materialistic reward.

America's "Industrial Age" in the 19th century created some of the country's first millionaires. Along with improved systems of transportation, communication, banking, machinery, and mass production came mass exploitation of poor men, women, and children. In a very real sense, the Puritans' benevolent wish for "better and richer and fuller" lifestyles for the common man evolved into an exclusive materialistic hymnal for the rich.

"There has been something crude and heartless and unfeeling in our haste to succeed and be great," President Woodrow Wilson declared in 1913 at the beginning of the 20th century—himself both a courageous critic of corporate power and exemplary racist and expander of the U.S. empire. "We have squandered a great part of what we might have used, and have not stopped to conserve the exceeding bounty of nature, without which our genius for enterprise would have been worthless and impotent."[17]

Vanity Fair's contributing editor, David Kamp, offered an excellent analysis of the genesis and transformation of the American Dream in "Rethinking the American Dream" (April 2009). By the start of World War II, Kamp noted how the tenets of the American Dream had been incorporated into the rallying cries for war.[18]

In his 1941 pre-war State of the Union address, Roosevelt declared that the United States would be fighting for: "freedom of speech and expression"; "freedom of every person to worship God in his own way"; "freedom from want"; and "freedom from fear."

Roosevelt upheld "the 'American way' as a model for other nations to follow," Kamp wrote, adding that Roosevelt also "presented the four freedoms not as the lofty principles of a benevolent super race but as the homespun, bedrock values of a good, hardworking, un-extravagant people."

Although the American Dream had been compromised by the rich and war-ready, it remained a symbol of basic freedoms and necessities. Thousands of returning veterans in 1944 were able to attend college and become homeowners, thanks to paid tuition and low-interest loans through the G.I. Bill. These benefits during "a severe housing shortage and a boom in young families," Kamp noted, led to the "rapid-fire development of suburbia."

Up until the late 1940s, the average white family's ideal aspirations were attainable. With a house; a car; and one working parent with a decent-paying, benefit-providing job; 20th-century Americans had a good shot at achieving a modest version of the American Dream.

Unfortunately, with the advent of television, the dream became a manipulative marketing tool used to spark unprecedented consumerism. With television programs as benchmarks, we can chart the public depictions of family, for example, from the working-class environment of Ralph and Alice in *The Honeymooners* to the opulent lifestyles of J. R. and his broods in the 1970s television show *Dallas*. Fast-forward three more decades,

and we're overwhelmed with a litany of lavish, deca-
dent, and over-indulgent unreal reality shows.

During the late 1950s, as televisions became more
affordable, credit cards also hit the consumer market.
Suddenly, a working-class society that had been used to
paying with cash had the ability to instantly obtain the
products, services, and luxuries beamed into their living
rooms every night.

Commenting on this societal shift of the late 1950s,
Kamp wrote:

> "What unfolded over the next generation was the
> greatest standard-of-living upgrade that this coun-
> try had ever experienced: an economic sea change
> powered by the middle class's newly sophisticated
> engagement in personal finance via credit cards,
> mutual funds, and discount brokerage houses—
> and its willingness to take on debt."[19]

The 21st-century American Dream had been defined
by wealth and unpredictable lottery-type success. Most
of us can't afford the looks and lifestyles of J-Lo, the Kar-
dashians, Sean (P-Diddy) Combs, or Justin Bieber. But,
with our credit cards in hand and a quick trip to the
nearest retail outlet, we think we can come darn close
with the purchase of their fragrances, jewelry, and clothing lines, as well as by donning their hair styles.

The 21st-century American Dream had been defined
by wealth, power, and success. Folks from humble backgrounds who get paid big time for writing best-selling
novels, making Oscar-winning films, excelling in golf,
winning the title of "American Idol," or becoming

President of the United States are said to have "achieved the American Dream."

For the rest of us, our parents' and grandparents' dream has become unattainable in the 21st century. Infected by the country's historic motto, we were duped into leveraging all in an illusory pursuit of a marketed "better and richer and fuller" life.

According to the "MetLife Study of the American Dream," released in 2011, Americans are at a crossroads. We are still "driven by one tenet of American progress—that hard work will get you ahead," but that belief has been shaken to the core by the intense economic downturn. According to the report, Americans are no longer seeking personal wealth; they are just looking for "a sense of financial security that allows them to live a sustainable lifestyle."[20]

If we are to get to a place of shared security, we must first confront some cold, hard facts. Our chickens have come home to roost. While we maligned and ignored the poor and worked to separate them from those more fortunate, poverty snaked its way into mainstream America. As unemployment, corporate greed, and the divide between the rich and the rest of us grew exponentially in the 21st century, we held onto our stale 20th century habits.

To get out of this economic mess, we must thoroughly dissect the missing pieces that placed almost 50 million of us in this calamitous position. Greedy and gluttonous individuals and institutions must be exposed and brought to justice. We have to dissect the poverty of collective actions and thought that got us into this predicament and vow to do better. Lastly, we must map out a bold and courageous path for change—by all means necessary.

After we've done these things and more—then and only then can we craft a truly equitable and inclusive course to the American Dream.

CHAPTER 2

Poverty of Opportunity

*"We can have democracy in this country,
or we can have great wealth concentrated
in the hands of a few, but we can't have both."*

—Louis D. Brandeis

He had the look of the "Marlboro Man" from the old cigarette TV commercials—tanned, weathered skin like cow leather, stubbly beard, and piercing blue eyes. Jack, a veteran honorably discharged in 1986 after serving almost ten years in the Navy, was rather gaunt. You could tell he hadn't had three squares in a long, long time.

We met Jack and other military veterans during our stop in Akron, Ohio. The Reverend Tom Gerstenlauer allowed us to gather at his church, Miller Avenue United, located in one of Akron's poorest neighborhoods. The racially diverse congregation is comprised of the working poor, homeless veterans, and single parents from the neighborhood.

By the size of his grizzled hands, it was apparent that Jack was no stranger to a hard day's work. Maybe alcohol or drugs played a part in his condition; he didn't say. However, we will never forget the story he decided to share—bravely— with us in the church's crowded rectory:

> "Yes, I'm Jack and I'm homeless. I sleep here and there, wherever I can bunk. I've worked all my life, but the way the economy is, there's no work out there for me now, and I'm not able to really work because I have so many disabilities—bad back, bad knees."

Jack told us he's still waiting to be approved for Social Security and disability payments. He had just missed an appointment when we were there in August 2011; he fears he'll have to wait another two years to get another chance to plead his case for government help.

The economy, Jack said, has left him in a bad way. He has a "legal situation" that includes child support payments that are a "little bit" late. The courthouse, he continued, is in Portage County, about 10 miles away from Akron.

> "I'm not able to get to Portage County because I'm unable to walk there, and I have no other way. That's putting me in jeopardy . . . it's threatening my life. I can easily be put in prison for this . . . and I don't want to be there."

Jack's not sure what sort of work his ailing body will allow him to do, but he's hoping some sort of work will come through so he won't have to keep living on the street or in homeless shelters.

"I just wish the jobs would come through . . . that Obama does what he says he's going to do to get us work. I hope I get my Social Security so I can take care of my Portage County problems. I just . . . I just don't know what else to say except . . . I'm kinda under a rock."

Jack's story underscores the extreme lack of opportunity in America. Our country, citizens, veterans, and our children are locked in situations of hopelessness. On the lopsided scales of justice, a tiny segment enriched by the majority of America's wealth has been elevated. On the other side, the scale has been weighted down by the rest—the struggling, the poor, the forgotten.

Share of total wealth gain, 1983-2009

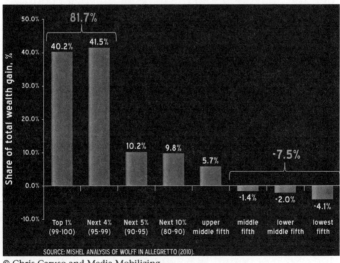

© Chris Caruso and Media Mobilizing
Graphic Design: Nate Adams and Mindi Mumaw

A surplus of opportunity comes in the form of economic equality. In this equation there are jobs with decent wages that give people like Jack a chance to breathe, to dream, to build, and to mend or maintain strong family and community bonds.

America is often regarded as "the greatest country" on earth, first among all Western nations and the leader of the free world.

But is this identity still true?

Can we still claim "the greatest" status when one out of two Americans is living in poverty or near the poverty line? Should our reputation as a global leader legitimately come into question when, every quarter, millions more of our citizens face the haunting specter that they, too, may soon join the ranks of America's poor?

How patriotic is a nation where veterans are more likely than non-veterans to be homeless? The National Coalition for Homeless Veterans estimates that more than 67,000 veterans are homeless on any given night, but about 1.5 million are considered at risk of homelessness due to poverty, lack of support networks, or dismal living conditions and substandard housing.[21]

What are the real choices and chances available in our democracy for average citizens when the wealthiest 1 percent of U.S. citizens controls nearly 42 percent of the wealth, or when the top 400 citizens have wealth equivalent to the bottom 150 million citizens? Is this still the land of real opportunity when nearly 14 million Americans are "officially" unemployed, and millions more are underemployed, to say nothing of the countless millions who have completely given up looking for work?

The myth of American exceptionalism, of being the best of the best, overshadows an inconvenient truth. We are a nation where poverty of opportunity is dangerously close to becoming a permanent reality.

The power of this myth stifles most of our leaders' abilities to even utter the "P" word in public. For decades, every President has stood before the American people and assured us that the "State of our Union is strong," despite years of convincing contradictory evidence, especially as it relates to poverty.

Although politicians hate to address poverty, the media are delving into the plight of the poor because the escalating numbers of the "new poor" and "near poor" are white citizens who are now struggling alongside long-suffering citizens of color.

Discussions of poverty, like the ones of once-verböten global warming, have finally moved into the public sphere. This is due in large part to the historic protests of the Occupy Wall Street movement. However, we refuse to allow poverty to become another topic du jour on mainstream media's drive through menu.

Why? Because like terrorism and the nation's deficit, poverty is a matter of national security. The current poverty numbers constitute a state of emergency in America, which means that ending poverty must become a top agenda item for all political leaders. There must be a constant drumbeat heard throughout the land about how widespread poverty is and why every citizen ought to have a sense of urgency about its eradication.

THE THREAT TO OUR NATION'S SECURITY

"Poverty in the United States is a moral and social
wound in the soul of our country. It is an ongoing
disaster that threatens the health and
well-being of our nation."
—Catholic Charities, 2006

A year before the recession was officially noted, Catholic Charities—one of the largest networks of social service providers in America—chastised political leaders for their "conscious and deliberate retreat from our nation's commitment to economic justice for those who are poor." Its policy paper, "Poverty in America: A Threat to the Common Good" (2006), expressed extreme disappointment with political efforts to dismantle safety nets that assist the impoverished. Because Catholic Charities believes that poverty remains our "most serious political blind spot," it issued a serious indictment:

> "We have the resources, experience, and knowledge to virtually eliminate poverty, especially long-term poverty, but we do not yet have the political will."[22]

Paving avenues to opportunity in tough times requires backbone and determinate will. Without them, our nation and its citizens will flounder.

THERE GOES THE NEIGHBORHOOD

Foreclosures were filed against 2.9 million American homeowners in 2010, and the numbers grew in 2011.

According to the U.S. Department of Housing and Urban Development (HUD), homeless families increased 28 percent, from 131,000 in 2007 to 168,000 in 2010. Additionally, based on data from HUD and the U.S. Department of Veterans Affairs, 67,495 veterans are homeless; 4,355 of them headed households with children.

Without jobs and opportunities, once-stable neighborhoods started to disintegrate. For the first time in decades, middle class suburbia began facing the same dilemma as long-neglected inner cities: an extended period of economic stagnation, which has bred family and community deterioration and despair.

In the summer of 2011, Kathryn Edin, Harvard professor of public policy and family expert, compiled research and conducted interviews in the middle class neighborhoods of Northeast and South Philadelphia. Her team noted rises in divorce, alcoholism, and violence, accompanied by the unraveling of the social fabric in the neighborhoods.

"These white working-class communities—once strong, vibrant, proud communities, often organized around big industries—they're just in terrible straits," Edin said.[23] "I hang around these neighborhoods in South Philadelphia, and I think, 'This is beginning to look like the Black inner-city neighborhoods we've been studying for the past 20 years.'" Even conservative figures like Charles Murray conclude that white working-class communities are in deep crisis.

Philadelphia isn't an anomaly. Poverty and unemployment are having a cancer-like effect on neighborhoods across the country. Many overleveraged properties

—multifamily dwellings and residential buildings dependent on renters to cover the mortgage payments and maintenance costs—have gone into foreclosure because more and more people can't afford to pay their rents.

The New York-based nonprofit, Citizens Housing and Planning Council, and Enterprise Community Partners commissioned a study to examine neighborhood deterioration as it relates to over-mortgaged buildings. More than 1,000 foreclosed properties in Manhattan, Queens, Brooklyn, and the Bronx within 250 to 500 feet of overleveraged properties were examined. The early 2012 study, "The Impact of Multifamily Foreclosures and Over-Mortgaging in Neighborhoods in New York City," revealed disturbing trends. Housing code violations of buildings near troubled properties were increasing at alarming rates. In other words, foreclosed properties are scaring neighboring property owners. Harold Shultz, senior fellow of the study, explains: "There is reason to believe that if a building is in trouble, other owners are dissuaded to make investment in their properties because they fear that it is not worth the investment."

When property owners sense decline, they stop investing, and maintenance of their properties goes by the wayside. City code violations increase, which leads to more foreclosures. Rental rates are lowered for low-income people, and all the social baggage that accompanies poverty invades previously stable neighborhoods. Like in the days of "white flight"—when white Americans exited the nation's cities based on negative perceptions of declining property values in racially mixed communities that led to self-filling prophecies—today's foreclosure crisis means that once-promising neighborhoods face the threat of becoming deteriorating slums.

President Obama, in his 2012 State of the Union address, announced a federal program to help struggling homeowners avoid foreclosures and save about $3,000 per year on their mortgages. According to several polls, the majority of Americans favored some kind of government intervention to prevent them from losing their homes through bank foreclosures. Politicians instead immediately dove into divisive partisan debates.

This was just another painful example of how the lack of political will threatens to forestall immediate opportunities to save homes, neighborhoods, and families.

SUFFER THE CHILDREN

"The greatest threat to America's national security comes from no enemy without but from our own failure to protect, invest in, and educate all of our children who make up all of our futures in this global economy."

—Marian Wright Edelman,
Children's Defense Fund founder

Quitman County, with its tiny population of about 8,000, has always been one of the poorest counties in the Mississippi Delta. The economic disparity and poverty in Quitman was so intense in 1967 that Dr. Martin Luther King, Jr., decided to kick off the Poor People's Campaign from there. A year before his death, in preparation for the event, King visited a ramshackle schoolhouse in the town of Marks, located in Quitman.

King was moved to tears as he watched a teacher feed children their lunch—crackers and a single apple sliced among them.

A few years ago, Marian Wright Edelman, founder of the Children's Defense Fund (CDF), commissioned Pulitzer Prize–winning author Julia Cass to go to the Mississippi Delta and other poverty-ridden counties and cities to find poor children "and tell their stories" for the CDF photo-essay report, "'Held Captive': Child Poverty in America" (2010).[24]

In Lambert, another small Quitman County town, Cass met Robert Jamison, founder and director of the North Delta Youth Development Center, a nonprofit center that offers afterschool programs for area children.

Jamison grew up in Quitman and has painful memories of 1960s–era racism. He was one of the first ten Black children to attend the all-white school in Marks, just two miles from Lambert. Jamison was harassed so much that he quit that same year and returned to his neighborhood Black school.

Today the county is too poor to afford segregation. Almost 30 percent of the families in Quitman live below the poverty line; children under the age of 18 comprise 43 percent of that number. In Quitman, poor white kids attend schools with poor Black kids. Jamison empathizes with the white kids:

"If you are a poor white here, you are the under, underdog," he said.

Chastity—a poor white child, Cass wrote, "who lives in a dilapidated house in Lambert, across the tracks in what used to be the all-white part of town"—is definitely an underdog. The shy and withdrawn girl—11 at the time of the interview—"gets along good" with other children at school, her grandmother says, but "she's behind." Chastity's mother lives in Batesville in Panola County, another part of Mississippi. Chastity has lived with her grandmother since the age of seven. Her grandmother cannot read or write and is unable to offer her granddaughter the help she needs with her schoolwork and other problems.

Jamison doesn't believe Chastity is as slow as people seem to think.

"Oh no, no, no. She's kind of on the shy side, but she's a smart young girl. She really wants to do better," said Jamison, who met Chastity when she came to his center seeking help. "She came and talked to me, asked could I talk to her grandmother because 'I need tutoring in math. I'm so behind.'"[25]

Chastity's real problem is generational poverty, Jamison explained. Chastity's grandmother, he told Cass, tries her best but doesn't understand the importance of education because, he said, "she never experienced anybody pushing her to go to school."

Quitman County and other towns in the Mississippi Delta are in dire need of funds for "special assistance to families," especially one-parent households, to improve the educational outcomes of impoverished children.

If education and educational support isn't available, Jamison believes impoverished, misdiagnosed, and potentially bright young children in Quitman, like Chastity, will be allowed to fall by the wayside.

"If you're a single parent trying to raise a family without resources, it's hell. Some places have people or companies who will sponsor a child, making sure they have uniforms and can take part in extracurricular activities. That means a lot to a child and gives them something to go out for and keep on going," Jamison added.

In this economy, the amount of women "without resources" has increased exponentially. In 2011, the poverty rate for women reached 16.2 percent compared to about 14 percent for men. This is the largest poverty rate increase for women in 17 years.

WOMEN & POVERTY

The poverty rate among women
rose from
13.9 percent in 2009
to
16.2 percent in 2010
the highest rate in 17 years.

The "extreme poverty rate" among women
also hit a record high, from
5.9 percent in 2009
to
6.3 percent in 2010.

Poverty Rate Nationally	15.1%
Poverty Rate among women	16.2%
Poverty Rate among men	14.0 %

Based 0n 2011 Census figures

Perhaps the nation's schools aren't all as bad as the ones in Quitman, but anybody who has paid attention knows that the poorer a child is in America, the more likely he or she is to be malnourished, misdiagnosed, and herded into over-crowded, under-funded, and poorly staffed educational institutions. While rich kids go off to college, America's poor children drop out of school, wind up in the nation's jails or prisons, or are destined to live the lives of the working poor—or worse.

There are almost 16 million children (15,749,129 or 21.6%) living in poverty according to the Children's Defense Fund. Of those, 7 million (9.6%) live in extreme poverty. Experts use the number of families receiving cash assistance from Temporary Assistance for Needy Families (TANF), the number of children who receive SNAP (food stamps), and the amount of children participating in the nation's school lunch programs to determine hunger in the United States. Almost 4.5 million adults and children receive TANF and more than 18.5 million children receive food stamps. More than 8.9 million women, infants, and children participate in the government's supplemental nutrition program, WIC.

Nearly 40 million depend on the nation's School Lunch Program for a healthy meal and sustenance at school.

**PORTRAIT OF CHILD POVERTY
IN THE UNITED STATES**

Number of poor children	15,749,129 (21.6%)
Number of children living in extreme poverty	7,023,152 (9.6%)
Number of adults and children receiving Temporary Assistance for Needy Families (TANF)	4,463,752
Number of children receiving food stamps (SNAP)	18,516,000
Number of children in the School Lunch Program	31,398,104
Number of women and children receiving WIC (Supplemental Nutrition Program)	8,905,676

One of the most damning indictments of our national priorities is the number of its impoverished and homeless children. The National Center on Family Homelessness (NCFH) reported in 2011 that 1 in 45, or 1.6 million, children were living on the street, in homeless shelters or motels, or doubled up with other families. This number represents a 33 percent increase from 2007, when there were 1.2 million homeless children, according to the NCFH report.[26]

The picture is even bleaker when we consider data from the Children's Defense Fund (CDF) and the Annie E. Casey Foundation.[27] The CDF's annual "State of America's Children" 2011 report detailed how the economic downturn shoved 15.5 million more children and families into poverty. Children of color, the report further explained, suffered disproportionately with more than 1 in 3 Black and 1 in 3 Hispanic children living in poverty compared to more than 1 in 10 white, non-Hispanic children.

Patrick McCarthy, president and CEO of the Annie E. Casey Foundation, talked about America's "huge, huge crisis" based on the unemployment and foreclosure figures in 2011 that were having such an adverse effect on our nation's children:

> "You've got almost half of the unemployed [who] have now been unemployed for more than six months, and they have children. "We're also seeing a huge impact of foreclosure on children. We're seeing 5.3 million children impacted by foreclosure between 2007 and 2009 alone . . . and that's also not counting those children who are impacted because the place where they live, their landlord was foreclosed upon and as renters they were forced to move out."

How can America be "first" if the least among us are our last collective concern? What does it say about the priorities of a nation that allows 53 percent of its children—the most vulnerable and valuable—to live in or near poverty?

We wholeheartedly agree with Edelman's assessment that our national security is in jeopardy until we invest in child health care, early childhood development, education, and other programs that save vulnerable young lives.

"God has blessed America with extraordinary

material wealth. America can and must step forward to correct the gross imbalance of government subsidization of the wealthiest and most powerful among us and provide a future for all children free from hunger, hopelessness, and despair," Edelman declares. "If America cannot stand up for its children, it does not stand for anything at all. And it will not stand strong in our competitive, global world."[28]

Something is profoundly wrong in America when the younger you are, the more likely you are to be poor. Therefore, we must stand. We cannot allow our children to surrender their life chances before they know their life choices.

As we noted in the previous chapter, President Franklin D. Roosevelt—influenced by his wife Eleanor—summoned the will to create programs that gave Great Depression–era Americans the opportunity to work and dream their way back to prosperity. In defining Roosevelt's "New Deal," historians often refer to the "3 R's" of his programs: "Relief, Recovery, and Reform." "Recovery" and "Reform" were all about repairing the economy and transforming a broken financial system. But the first "R" related to "Relief" for the unemployed and poor.

Roosevelt introduced a new poverty paradigm into politics that impacted succeeding administrations for more than 40 years. The storybook that is history reveals the chapters where a promising path took a disturbing detour.

SHORT-LIVED OPPORTUNITY

Harry S. Truman, President Franklin D. Roosevelt's third vice president, succeeded to the office of President less than three months after FDR's untimely death in 1945. Although Truman passed only one additional New Deal program during his two terms, he did not attempt to reverse any of his predecessor's liberal policies. On the domestic front, Truman delegated many duties to his cabinet while he focused on foreign and military affairs: ending racial discrimination in the armed forces; Nazi Germany's defeat; the use of nuclear weapons against Japan, implementing the Marshall Plan; creating the United Nations and NATO; containing communism, defrosting the Cold War; and closely monitoring the Chinese Civil War, the Korean War, and more, which consumed his tenure in office.

Five-star General Dwight D. Eisenhower campaigned against "Communism, Korea, and corruption," and his crusade paid off when he was elected the first Republican President since Herbert Hoover's election in 1929. Opponents of The New Deal Coalition—a strong alliance of Democratic Party affiliates, labor unions, blue-collar workers, intellectuals, people on relief, minorities, and others—considered Eisenhower's victory an opportunity to champion their "less government" agendas. Their expectations weren't met. Eisenhower, whom historians regard as a "moderate conservative," didn't challenge New Deal legislation and, in fact, continued funding most agencies founded by FDR.

The virulent 1960s were also marked with courageous, inspirational leadership and historic change.
With the dawn of the new decade, Americans elected
the first president born within the 20th century and the
second-youngest (43) since Theodore Roosevelt.

By the time John F. Kennedy entered office in 1960,
The New Deal Coalition was severely fractured. New,
contentious issues of the times—the Vietnam War, race
relations, riots, and activists' demands for civil rights
and affirmative action—drove many members of Congress in different directions. These issues, when mixed
with escalating confrontations with the Soviet Union
and the growing popularity of Republican candidates
who promised lower taxes and control of inner-city
crime, hampered Kennedy's efforts to repair the splin-
tered coalition.

However, reunification became Lyndon B. Johnson's
mission after Kennedy's assassination on November 22,
1963. President Johnson worked hard to reestablish the
liberal coalition, but with his brusque Texas style, he
wound up driving a bigger wedge into the legislature.
Undeterred, and inspired by Harrington's definitive book
on poverty, Johnson declared a "War on Poverty" during
his first State of the Union address on January 8, 1964.[29]

It was more than feel-good rhetoric. Johnson backed
his declaration with a series of bills and acts, such as
food stamps, Head Start, work study, Job Corps, Medicaid, and Medicare to bring about real results for improving the standard of living for America's poor. The endur-
ing legacy of Johnson's "Great Society" was the belief
that government should play a role and use education,

health care, and other proactive federal programs such as the *Economic Opportunity Act of 1964* to enact poverty reduction.

With 1964 poverty rates of about 19 percent nationally and almost double that number in most Black households, Johnson faced a daunting task. Yet progress was made. For instance, by 1969, after passage of the *Civil Rights Act of 1964*, the *Economic Opportunity Act of 1964*, and the *Voting Rights Act of 1965*, the Black poverty rate fell from a 41.8 percent high in 1966 to 32.2 percent by 1969. More importantly, Johnson demonstrated the will to stand against poverty, which remained a major part of political discourse after his term. Unfortunately, that discourse wasn't always progressive.

BLACKLASH

"If any man claims the Negro should be content . . .
let him say he would willingly change the color
of his skin and go to live in the Negro section
of a large city. Then and only then
has he a right to such a claim."
—Senator Robert F. Kennedy

During the 1968 presidential campaign, Democratic presidential candidate Robert Kennedy toured the country addressing poverty and highlighting the inequities between the rich and the poor. In 1967, Dr. King's protégé, Marian Wright, who headed the NAACP Legal Defense and Educational Fund in Mississippi at the time, invited Kennedy to follow King's pilgrimage and come see the reality of rural poverty in the Mississippi Delta.

After visiting Mississippi, Appalachia, and urban ghettos and witnessing children with "bellies swollen with hunger" and unable to go to school for lack of clothes or shoes, Kennedy vowed to introduce legislation that would remedy poverty and hunger.

Even Kennedy's opponent, Richard Nixon, gave a laissez-faire but notable nod to poverty during his Republican nomination speech. Nixon said that as President, he didn't promise to "eradicate poverty," but he could promise action and new policies "for peace and progress and justice at home."[30]

The argument of many conservatives and some white middle-class bigots that the War on Poverty gave special attention and perks to Blacks, specifically, fueled a backlash that helped Nixon win the 1969 presidential contest.

Historians define Nixon as a centrist politician who greatly expanded the 1964 *Food Stamp Act* and initiated job training, employment programs, and legislation that created openings for minorities on federally funded construction projects. However, Nixon's administration is also marred by his unofficial policy of "benign neglect."[31] New York Senator Daniel Patrick Moynihan —an urban affairs adviser to the White House staff at the time—proposed this benign neglect policy that was widely regarded as a cooling-off period for "Negro progress." Moynihan's memos stated that "the issue of race could benefit from a period of 'benign neglect,' which seemed to encourage an abandonment of urban (particularly Black) neighborhoods." Based on inaccurate information, Moynihan assumed that fires and "widespread arson" in poverty-stricken, Black majority neighborhoods like the South Bronx or Harlem were the work of Black arsonists or rioters. Moynihan suggested that fire departments no longer engage in the so-called futile war against arson and remarked that cities would benefit from such benign neglect.

By 1970, the poverty rate had dropped to about 12 percent. It fluctuated between 11 and 13 percent throughout the terms of Nixon and President Gerald Ford, who was appointed after Nixon's resignation—a direct result of the Watergate scandal in 1974. Ford's minimal impact on poverty was further overshadowed by his controversial pardon of Nixon, a weak economy, growing inflation, and a recession (1973–75) that signaled the end of the post–World War II boom.

Throughout President Jimmy Carter's term (1977–81), he was overwhelmed by an economic crisis produced by rising energy prices and, later, several major international political crises: the 1979 takeover of the American embassy in Iran; an unsuccessful rescue attempt of the hostages taken during the coup; the Soviet invasion of Afghanistan; and a crashing economy on the home front.

To his credit, Carter—who came into office with the promise of a "competent and compassionate" administration—tried to tackle what he considered the nation's larger, more spiritual problems. In his bold and intricate July 1979 "Crisis of Confidence" speech, he challenged the country to examine and rise above its materialistic mind-set:

"In a nation that was proud of hard work, strong families, close-knit communities, and our faith in God, too many of us now tend to worship self-indulgence and consumption. Human identity is no longer defined by what one does, but by what one owns."[32]

The sense of humanity and social responsibility that Carter encouraged took on a different tone after his term ended in defeat. As economist Jeffrey Sachs pointed out during an interview on *Tavis Smiley* on PBS, the 1980s introduced a dramatic and calculated shift in the War on Poverty:

"But then came [President Ronald] Reagan and the backlash . . . when Ronald Reagan came into office, and he came into office on a platform that said government is not the solution, it's the problem. . . . He started to dismantle. He gave tax cuts to the rich, started to cut the base out of our education spending, social safety net; [he] stopped investing in infrastructure—the things that make America productive."[33]

Reagan was "no friend to America's cities or its poor," Peter Dreier, chair of the Urban & Environmental Policy Department at Occidental College, boldly asserted in a commentary shortly after the former President's death.

"Reagan came to office in 1981 with a mandate to reduce federal spending. In reality, he increased it through the escalating military budget, all the while slashing funds for domestic programs that assisted working-class Americans, particularly the poor."[34]

Although most conservatives—desperate to gold-plate Reagan's legacy—boast that he restored the nation's prosperity, he did so at the expense of the poor.

"The income gap between the rich and everyone else in America widened," Dreier continued. "Wages for the average worker declined and the nation's homeownership rate fell. During Reagan's two terms in the White House, which were boom times for the rich, the poverty rate in cities grew."[35]

The goal here is not to solely criticize Reagan or Republicans. It is to chart the War on Poverty's timeline and pinpoint the myopic moment when anti-poor rhetoric and subsequent legislation turned stereotypical, vicious, and punitive. Reagan was more than the general who waved the white flag of surrender in the War on Poverty; he actually initiated the "War on Welfare." He was also the architect of "trickle-down" economics—a theory based on the false notion that tax policies that benefit the wealthy will magically lift the poor.

Some of the most devastating conditions that the poor face today are legacies of the Reagan era. Reagan slashed the budgets for so-called entitlement programs such as Medicaid, food stamps, the Environmental Protection Agency, Community Development Block Grants, and federal education programs by 60 percent. He froze the minimum wage at $3.35 an hour and cut public housing and Section 8 rent subsidies by 50 percent. As Dreier noted in his commentary, the number of homeless people—among them Vietnam veterans, children, and laid-off workers—swelled to 1.2 million under Reagan's watch. We suppose that the late Robert Lekachman was right in the best book written on Reaganomics, *Greed Is Not Enough.*[36]

Reagan may have set the tone and tenor for today's political conversations on poverty, but President Bill Clinton, during his administration (1993–2000), became a surprising conductor of the right-wing's "punish the poor" orchestra. In the runup to his re-election in 1996, Clinton out-GOP'd the GOP by signing a draconian welfare-to-work reform bill. Although the legislation reduced the numbers on welfare, it pushed unskilled people into a workforce that had no use for them. The effort may have helped win an election, but it reduced poverty by only 2.5 percent—from 13.7 percent in 1996 to 11.2 percent in 2000.

Ronald Reagan may have shifted the dialogue and outreach to the poor, but what's amazing, as Jeffrey Sachs noted during the PBS interview, is that the dialogue of denial, denigration, and dismissal of the poor continued throughout the Clinton administration: "The Bush era with more tax cuts, and tragically, it's continued through the first years of the Obama administration."

JUST THE FACTS

Before the Great Recession, roughly 37 million Americans were living in poverty. That number has soared to almost 50 million today, according to the most recent revised Census numbers. At the time of this writing, nearly 14 million Americans were unemployed, and millions more were under-employed. Again, this number does not reflect those who are no longer looking for work. Despite reports of the stock market's recovery, it remains harder than ever to find work in America, and for many of the working poor, having a job is just not enough. As corporate profits soared, middle class jobs vanished. High-wage industries accounted for only 14 percent of new jobs, while low-wage work made up almost 50 percent of the job growth. The average high-wage job pays between $17.43 to $31 an hour. On the other hand, low- to mid-wage jobs pay between $8.92 to $15 an hour, which is well below the national average hourly wage of $22.60.

In 2010, close to 9 million people were working part-time only because they could not find full-time employment. America is experiencing the highest rate of long-term unemployment in a generation, with almost half of the unemployed looking for work for more than six months.

Over the past 40 years, household incomes have remained stagnant for all but the top 5 percent of Americans, whose incomes skyrocketed over the same period. The Pew Research Center reported in 2011 that Black and Hispanic families have suffered most, with Black families losing 53 percent of their wealth and Hispanic families losing 66 percent of theirs by 2009.

The sobering reality is that without conscious and immediate intervention, America may soon be saddled with a new class, the "permanently poor." In advance of "The Poverty Tour: A Call to Conscience," we commissioned the Indiana University (IU) School of Public and Environmental Affairs to examine the recession and its after-effects on poverty. The findings, released in January 2012, are stunning. IU's White Paper, "At Risk: America's Poor During and After the Great Recession," underscores how the recession has left behind the largest number of "long-term unemployed" since 1948. It concludes that the "well-being of low-income Americans, particularly the working poor, the near poor, and the new poor, are at substantial risk," despite politicians' and Wall Street's declarations of an economic recovery.[37]

With the economic reality that real wages for the American working class have not increased for the past four decades, it is past time to challenge the distorted language and accompanying political rhetoric about the poor. We must move past Republican and Democratic versions of trickle-down economics—the belief that helping the rich and middle classes will magically improve the lot of the poor and working poor. Job growth has stalled so badly that several economists predict that, even if the economy rebounds, unemployment levels by the end of 2013 may return only to 2007 levels—around 4.6 percent, or almost 14 million people.

Both major political parties know that there will be no quick economic turnaround. The hard truth is we're going to be wrestling with unprecedented economic conditions for years to come. Yet, neither Democrats nor Republicans have a plan to address the proven factors that underlie intractable poverty.

Those who control America's purse strings must be called out on the disingenuous and deceitful language used when they (rarely) broach the subject: Talk of a great economic comeback based on "minimum wage" jobs as opposed to "living wage" jobs; a "jobless recovery" without a "job-based recovery" plan and process; helping the "working poor" without a solid roadmap to help "poor people" find a way out of poverty. The lack of concrete, unequivocal, direct language employed when we try to address these problems underscores a lack of will and the political inability to provide real opportunities for the poor.

We must reject this cynical and manipulative vocabulary and demand a more honest and ethical language that does not beat down the poor or trivialize poor people's pain and suffering.

With strategically planned and innovative efforts to vastly cut or completely eliminate America's social and economic safety nets—food stamps, Medicaid, unemployment insurance, federal housing, and educational assistance—poverty will become the new American "normal."

As we've seen in societies all over the world, chaos reaches a tipping point when there are no options or solutions for economic salvation. History has taught us that there is no empire in the world that did not at some point decline or fall. Every empire, especially shortsighted societies that catered to greedy and powerful rulers and dictators at the expense of the poor, eventually crumbled.

As hard as it is for us to accept, with the rich getting richer, the poor getting poorer, and the class divide getting wider, there is very little reason not to believe that America could one day implode under the weight of escalating poverty.

In America, as in Africa, Europe, and the Middle East, we are witnessing a magnificent democratic awakening with restless citizens all around the world demanding justice. We have rightly celebrated the democratic uprisings in Egypt, Tunisia, Yemen, and elsewhere without realizing that *economic injustice* is just as explosive on our own soil. *Can poverty be the spark that ignites democratic enlightenment?*

The American Dream has inspired progressive change all over the world. There is sad irony in that the loss of this over-mortgaged dream is now igniting protests on our own soil.

Alexis de Tocqueville was the first major commentator to describe the United States as "exceptional." To be sure, America is unique and distinctive. But as Frederick Douglass opined, a true patriot also must wrestle with the night side of democracy in America.

In 43 years, we have gone from an aggressive stance on the eradication of poverty to passive, indifferent, and downright destructive positions where the poor are maligned and rendered invisible. Because both major political parties are so dependent on big campaign contributions from the rich who benefit from loopholes and tax breaks, politicians are hesitant or lack the will to even utter the "P" word in the public sphere.

Put simply, when we make anything a priority in Washington, it gets done. We prioritized funding the wars in Iraq and Afghanistan and—bam!—it was done. We prioritized bailing out Wall Street; it was a done deal. Since there are no lobbyists for the poor lined up on K Street in the nation's capital, it is incumbent that the eradication of poverty be reintroduced into the national dialogue and that we force our leaders to make poor people a national priority again.

Being poor is six dollars short on the utility bill and no way
  to close the gap.
Being poor is crying when you drop the mac and cheese on the floor.
Being poor is knowing you work as hard as anyone, anywhere.
Being poor is people surprised to discover you're not actually stupid.
Being poor is people surprised to discover you're not actually lazy.
Being poor is a six-hour wait in an emergency room with a
  sick child asleep on your lap.
Being poor is never buying anything someone else hasn't bought first.

Being poor is knowing where the shelter is.
Being poor is people who have never been poor wondering why
  you choose to be so.
Being poor is knowing how hard it is to stop being poor.
Being poor is seeing how few options you have.
Being poor is running in place.
Being poor is people wondering why you didn't leave.

Excerpted from "Being Poor" by John Scalzi

Unless and until we rethink, re-imagine, and redefine how we confront poverty, it will never be eradicated. Unless and until we honestly tackle the greed and dissect the political, economic, and societal black holes that allow it to flourish, increasing and intractable poverty will remain American capitalism's and the global economy's permanent partner.

CHAPTER 3

Poverty of Affirmation

"I am invisible; understand, simply because people refuse to see me . . . When they approach me they see only my surroundings, themselves, or figments of their imagination— indeed, everything and anything except me."

—Ralph Ellison

Columbus, Mississippi, resident Brenda Caradine couldn't believe her eyes. She was working out on a treadmill at the local YMCA when, out the window, she saw a huge, white bus pulling up to the nearby Court Square Towers building. Emotions rising, Caradine read the blue and burgundy words on the mobile billboard: "The Poverty Tour: A Call to Conscience."

It was a "miracle from God," she'd later tell reporters. As it turns out, days earlier when Caradine learned the tour was headed to Columbus, she had written a protest letter to *The Commercial Dispatch,* the local newspaper. Caradine, a long-time supporter of the arts and head of the Tennessee Williams Festival, wrote that she wasn't at all pleased about the scheduled visit to Columbus.

The letter was never published.

So when the bus actually pulled up, Caradine ran outside and waited. She was anxious to read us the riot act. And she did. She did not appreciate the fact that we were in Columbus and she did not like the word "Poverty" emblazoned in huge letters on our bus.

"You're stigmatizing our town; this is not a poverty town," Caradine complained. "Why are you in Columbus? Why are you here?"

On and on she went, expressing her displeasure, and that's putting it kindly. We listened courteously, knowing that her sentiments are shared by many fellow citizens.

Affirming poor people is dangerous. It means that you first acknowledge their existence. Acknowledging the poor opens the door to perilous thoughts. We are forced to consider: "Can it happen to me?"

To many, poverty is regarded as a personal declaration of failure, a measure of fundamental unworthiness, or, as in Caradine's case, a blight on an upstanding community.

The truth about poverty must be affirmed. Like a man with a knife in his back staggering along a crowded street without aid, the poor have been stabbed with the blade of indifference. With a profusion of affirmation, we acknowledge the pain and rush to stop the bleeding. Affirmation leads to validation, which compels us to action.

The poor have long been maligned, stereotyped, and disgraced as lazy, irresponsible leeches who are a detriment to society. Politicians have color-coded poverty, making it a Black or brown thing. Against such a biased backdrop, it's understandable why people with personal and civic pride vehemently resist the "poverty" label.

Our only wish was that Caradine could have been with us when we visited Prairie Opportunity, Inc., in her town. The nonprofit agency provides services to low-income, elderly, disabled, and unemployed families. It helps them survive the tough times and, hopefully, rise to a point of self-sufficiency.

In this recession economy, Prairie Opportunity has been challenged with rapidly rising caseloads and massive budget cuts. The agency, in partnership with other nonprofits, serves eight counties within Mississippi's "Golden Triangle." The need is great and the money is tight. During our visit, directors told us that their federally funded 2011 budget of $2 million was slated to be slashed in 2012 to $800,000.

If Caradine had come with us, she would have come face to face with the poverty in her town. Joann Cotton would have made sure of it.

"I have a marketing degree. I've been unemployed for three years. My husband is disabled; he retired after 30 years because he has severe degenerative discs. We went from making $60,000 a year to less than $15,000 overnight. We are fighting foreclosure . . . it's hard, very, very hard."

Cotton's husband has several ailments, including emphysema. He doesn't get all his medication because "we can't afford it . . . we just get some," she said.

The couple receives food stamps "which is depressing as hell"—but perhaps not as depressing as her job search. The price of gas has made getting to interviews more than challenging. Cotton says she's filled out at least 300 job applications. She's even been called in for interviews. At 54, she believes her age is a detriment. Interviewers always compliment her years of experience but they never call back. "I just know they're going to hire someone 25 or 26 and not pay them as much," Cotton explained with evident frustration.

"I can do anything. I've opened clothing stores, I've managed, and I spent 16 years as an administrative assistant. All I want to do is get my foot in the door. Let me work."

Caradine thought the word "poverty" on our bus might bring shame or disrepute to her town. It's unfortunate that "appearances" were a greater concern to her than the badge of near despair that people like Cotton must wear as they battle the complexities of being unexpectedly cast in the role of America's new poor.

"I've aged 10 years in the three years that I've been looking for a job. My emotions are on high; my sense of humor is gone. You have no energy, you can't do anything," Cotton told us. "I'd like to exhale. I want to get a job so I can just relax and exhale . . . but I can't. After a while you just give up."

Empathizing with the psychological toll that poverty takes on the poor is impossible if we pretend it's not in our midst. To be poor is to enter a world of harsh judgment and an instant demotion in social stature. Not only is the humanity of the poor not affirmed, the poor are condemned. During our nationally televised "Remaking America" symposium in January 2012, panelist and distinguished author Barbara Ehrenreich talked about a system designed to demoralize the poor:

> "I would say the surprising, shocking, disgusting thing is that not only do we not help people who are having trouble or are sliding down, we kick them a little further. The whole system is rigged so that if you start to spiral down, you're going to spiral faster. There's no ladder going up. There's a greased chute going down."[38]

The conversation with Caradine and others on the tour gave us a sense of the level of denial that we're actually up against in this country. With poverty as a distasteful afterthought, how do we paint a true picture of what it really means to be human and poor in America? Is it even possible to get folk to stop treating poverty like it's a contagious disease to be avoided at all costs and instead to affirm the dignity and humanity of the poor? How do we lift Americans in need out of economic deprivation if we are unable to separate poverty fiction from poverty fact?

HOW POVERTY BECAME A DIRTY WORD

Americans' perceptions about poverty and the government's response to them have shifted numerous times between the elections of Franklin D. Roosevelt and Barack Obama. One of the boldest denunciations of the poor was blasted via television in 1984 when "the great communicator," President Ronald Reagan, gave his assessment during a live segment of *Good Morning America:*

"What we have found in this country, and maybe
we're more aware of it now, is one problem that
we've had, even in the best of times, and that is
the people who are sleeping on the grates, the
homeless who are homeless, you might say, by
choice."[39]

We don't think John, a Vietnam-era veteran we met
at Freedom House—a transitional shelter for homeless
veterans in Akron, Ohio—would agree that he had a
"choice" in the circumstances that left him poor, di-
vorced, and homeless.

"You talk about poverty. . . . I had a job, a family, the
car, the whole bit . . . everything a person's supposed to
have. Now, I'm down to nothing. Because I didn't have
the job, I lost my home. Because of losing my home . . .
my wife and me . . . well, we split up; we've been separated for over nine months now."

John—bespectacled, barrel-shaped, with a Colonel
Sanders–type goatee—shared an experience that was
echoed a lot as we trekked across America.

"I've been in retail for almost 30 years, working for
one of the major retail chains that decided they had to
close 140 stores," John continued. "I worked with people
who've been with the company 30, 40 years—some who
were a year or two or three away from collecting their
pensions and were looking forward to retirement. All of
a sudden everything was pulled out from under us."

John's financial free fall may make him look like a
casualty of the 21st century's Great Recession, but his
fate was actually sealed decades before when President
Reagan went from acknowledging the plight of the poor

to actually attacking them. Who could forget the President's stump speeches where he regaled crowds with the story of the so-called Chicago welfare queen? Journalists tried—in vain—to find the Cadillac-driving welfare cheat Reagan described who used more than 80 aliases, false addresses, and the names of nonexistent or dead husbands to steal $180,000 in government aid. The story was as suspect as Reagan's compassion for the downtrodden. He used a blatant stereotype of a conniving, lazy welfare cheat to justify cuts to programs that help poor men, women, and especially children. But, perhaps even more insidious, the master actor managed to steer the time machine back to the 19th century, when being poor was indeed a criminal offense.[40]

TO CATCH A THIEF

Methods to control welfare fraud are as old as the system itself. Part of President Johnson's Great Society programs included the creation of the Aid to Families with Dependent Children, or the AFDC program. For the first time, poor mothers—who were not elderly or disabled—were able to receive government stipends and food stamps. Along with the new program came a litany of stringent rules and regulations that at one time included "midnight raids" to make sure no man was in a home receiving welfare.

President Richard M. Nixon coined the phrase "War on Drugs" to define his initiative to crack down on rampant drug use not on the streets but in the military. But by the mid-1980s, the domestic application of the "war" was concentrated in mostly poor Black neighborhoods.

Through high-profile media stories about "welfare moms" caught using or selling drugs, "welfare" suddenly became synonymous with "illegal drugs." Policies became even more punitive, and the boundaries between the welfare system and the criminal justice system began to fade.

Welfare recipients began to be treated like liars and cheats before they ever received a single government welfare check. As technology has evolved, personal information and photographs are taken and entered into the government's database. Social Security numbers and other information are collected and cross-checked with other databases to make sure the potential recipient doesn't have a criminal record, outstanding arrest warrants, drug-related charges, or other convictions. Welfare recipients' lives are shockingly scrutinized. In many states, plain-clothes investigators, empowered by the local prosecutor's office and social workers, can perform degrading home visits without the recipient's permission in which the recipient feels guilty until able to prove herself innocent.

"If you go out now to get a job, a low-wage job around $8, $9 an hour, you are going to be drug tested, personality tested," Ehrenreich explained.[41] "All the questions are going to be whether you like to steal, whether you like to sell cocaine in the break room, things like that. There is the idea that if you are poor, there's something wrong with you, and you should probably end up incarcerated."[42]

Political historians say Reagan's fictitious "welfare queen" was really just a composite of welfare fraud cases that predated his presidential run. By associating welfare with immorality, dishonesty, and criminality, Reagan posthumously bears responsibility for normalizing the criminalization of low-income women of color.

From a historical vantage point, we understand Brenda Caradine's strong reaction to the word "poverty" on our bus. The subliminal aura of drugs and crime was not something she wanted associated with her town. Sadly, townsfolk have to grapple with the literal meaning of poverty.

With race-baiting divisiveness an ever-present weapon in the arsenal, protectors of the wealthy are very skilled in depicting the poor as prone to violence if they aren't given their government handouts. Consider Rush Limbaugh's August 8, 2011, rant as he responded to Cornel's comments during the Poverty Tour about affirming, acknowledging, and respecting poor people:

> "Okay, so how do you 'treat poor and working people with dignity' now? You give them their stuff . . . What does he [West] mean by this? He means they better get their stuff! They better get their stuff! If they don't get their stuff, it ain't gonna be about love; it's gonna be revenge and hatred. We all gonna go under if the poor people and the working people aren't given their dignity now."[43]

We'd like to remind our dear, dear brother Rush Limbaugh of Gandhi's words, "Poverty is the worst form of violence."

A DAY IN THE LIFE

With a pledge to "end welfare as we know it," former President Bill Clinton disappointed many, including us, by signing the *Personal Responsibility and Work Opportunity Reconciliation Act* in 1996. The ballyhooed welfare reform bill, which was really just a page out of the Republicans' "Contract With America" playbook, was Clinton's calculated compromise with the Republican-controlled Congress that, at the time, wanted to drastically overhaul, if not eliminate, the traditional welfare system.[44]

AFDC was replaced with TANF, or Temporary Assistance for Needy Families, a cumbersome bureaucratic system that prohibited unconditional entitlement and mandated time limits in which recipients must seek work.

Although lauded as a major success by some because it did actually kick people off welfare, critics like political scientist Joe Soss of the University of Minnesota–Twin Cities noted how it widened the gap between the rich and the poor:

> "Welfare reform has coincided with massive growth in income and wealth disparities; it has done little to slow the expansion of inequality and may have actually accelerated the trend. Has welfare reform created job opportunities for the poor? Has it promoted wages that allow low-wage workers to escape poverty? In both of these areas, the economic story remains the same: We have

little evidence that reform has produced achievements that warrant the label of success."[45]

As of June 2011, almost 4.5 million Americans were receiving TANF funds, an increase of almost 700,000 during the same period in 2008, when 3,732,253 Americans received such funds. For the first time in the history of the program, middle class whites now find themselves dependent on a humiliating system engineered for low-income people of color—a system where they are presumed to be criminals in the home and the workforce.

Instead of acknowledging and addressing the growing needs of poor families struggling in the quake of a recession, legislators implemented drastic nationwide cuts to the TANF program. According to a 2011 report issued by the Center on Budget and Policy Priorities, the slashing of TANF funds caused further hardship for 700,000 families, including 1.3 million children. While the job crisis continues, the report points out, "States are terminating or reducing benefits for some of the most vulnerable families, most of whom have very poor labor market prospects."[46]

When we dare to affirm the existence of poverty in our midst, we confirm reality; we take the first step necessary to ratify the necessity of change.

REAGAN'S GHOST

Today, the Reagan-era style of some 30 years ago that endorsed attacks on the poor is back in vogue. For example, consider the 2012 Republican nomination candidates who didn't hesitate to throw meat to their base by using a wide array of racial stereotypes and callous language to demonstrate their willingness to destroy the welfare system.

Candidate Herman Cain chose the "blame-the-victim" retort when responding to charges from the Occupy Wall Street movement that unemployment and poverty were largely the result of government deregulation, unchecked greed, and economic inequality:

"Don't blame Wall Street, don't blame the big banks," Cain boasted. "If you don't have a job and you are not rich, blame yourself!"

During a campaign stop in Iowa, former Pennsylvania Senator Rick Santorum received raucous applause with this zinger: "I don't want to make Black people's lives better by giving them somebody else's money."

Former Massachusetts Governor Mitt Romney, who repeatedly accused President Obama of transforming America into an "entitlement society" in early 2012, audaciously declared: "I'm not concerned about the very poor. We have a safety net there."[47]

Santorum corrected himself. He really meant to say "people," not "Black people," he said. Romney tried to massage his insensitivity in later interviews by admitting "it's not good being poor" while still stressing his main concern was helping the struggling middle class.

Candidate Newt Gingrich, like a pit bull with a juicy

steak bone clamped in his jaws, kept slamming minorities and the poor with insults that ranged from suggesting poor Black kids become school janitors, to labeling Obama the "food stamp President," to the demeaning observation that poor people should "want paychecks, not handouts"—as if they don't.

If Romney, Gingrich, Santorum, or any other clueless politician who demeans poor folk had joined us during the Prairie Opportunity gathering, they might have garnered a better understanding of what so-called poor people really want.

Cornel has a favorite phrase from Ralph Ellison: *"The blues ain't nothing but a personal catastrophe expressed lyrically."* With the voice of a chain-smoking bluesman, Mississippi resident, Early Robinson shared his blues.

"I'm an ex-military man. My wife is here," Early said, motioning across the room at his wife Christine. "We've been all over Columbus, Mississippi, trying to get some help. We both lost our jobs in the same month, ah, say . . . February 2011. We've had to pawn cars, do everything . . . I'm cutting grass and doing everything I can . . . this is how we can keep from losing our house. Can't get no assistance nowhere. I will be 54 years old. I'm strong, healthy, and got all kinds of skills . . . nobody's just not hiring."

The Robinsons are having a tough time adjusting to the economic downturn and to the stigma of being poor. The proud couple received welfare payments but had been cut off, Christine said, "because we made $2 too much."

When she started to cry, Early comforted her, "Baby, don't do that." The tears trickled anyway as Christine made a plea for employment:

"I worked with Alzheimer's patients, I have a CDL license, I can do just about anything, and I'm willing to do it . . . we have a 14-year-old son. Our life insurance is gone, car insurance gone, cable is gone, they came and turned the gas off last week. We have each other, we have God, and we just keep on going . . . but no one knows how you living."

It's true. Most folk really don't know what it's like to be poor in 21st century America unless they've lived the life. Most Americans choose instead to segregate themselves from poverty. The stereotypes and stigmas serve as curtains that separate "us" from "them." Politicians and their rich benefactors understand this inherent need, so they supply their supporters with enough emotional ammunition and distorted facts to make certain that no light shines through the curtain.

WHAT POOR?

The Heritage Foundation recently released its "What Is Poverty in the United States Today?" report.[48] Because the average poor American household has "luxuries" such as a microwave oven, air conditioning, cable TV, and Xbox video game consoles, the conservative think tank argued that "poor" really isn't poor in America.

In a cold-hearted attempt to shrink social services for the poor and lower taxes for the rich, the foundation ignored Census figures about the working poor, near poor, and new poor and zeroed in on material goods as a non-indicator of poverty. The report doesn't even attempt to distinguish if the items were new or used, owned or rented, or if they were purchased before or after people fell in or out of poverty.

According to government criteria, a family of four, living off less than $22,400 annually, fits the poverty standard—period. What does that amount mean to the average impoverished family? Perhaps breaking it down annually will give us a clearer picture.

According to the U.S. Department of Agriculture, a "moderately priced" plan to feed a family of four (two adults and two children between the ages of two and five) would cost about $193 per week or $10,036 per year. Let's say the family lived in a slum neighborhood paying rent of $500 per month. That's another $6,000. Add a modest amount of $300 for monthly utilities (heat, phone, electricity), and that's another $3,600. Let's pretend this was a family of frugal shoppers who spent only $1,000 the entire year for clothing. In our scenario, the typical poor family managed to get by on $20,636.00.[49]

According to the Heritage Foundation, the poor aren't really poor because they have a whopping annual bounty of $1,764 to splurge on video games, microwaves, and cable TV. The money couldn't possibly go toward things like transportation to and from work, medicine, insurance, and other priorities.

During a September 2011 interview on MSNBC, Rep. John Fleming (R-La.) criticized President Obama's proposed tax increases on the wealthy. With a completely straight face, Fleming, a member of Rep. Michele Bachmann's Tea Party Caucus, had the audacity to use his own congressional salary of $174,000 plus the $6.3 million he'd accrued in personal investments that year to whine about how Obama tax hikes would raise his taxes.

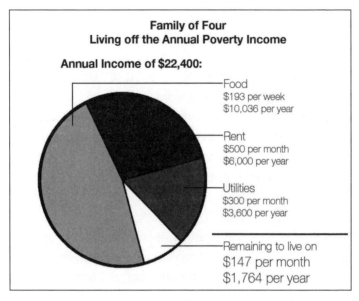

**Family of Four
Living off the Annual Poverty Income**

Annual Income of $22,400:

Food
$193 per week
$10,036 per year

Rent
$500 per month
$6,000 per year

Utilities
$300 per month
$3,600 per year

Remaining to live on
$147 per month
$1,764 per year

Based on data from the U.S. Census Bureau

Bruce Watson, a features writer for *Daily Finance,* took Fleming to task. Taking into account what the Congressman said he'd spent on staffing, equipment, investments, and various other business expenses, Watson deduced that Fleming had about $200,000 left over just to feed his family of four. Using calculations similar to ours, Watson concluded that Fleming's yearly food budget was "more than the total take-home salary for four average families making the median household income of $49,455.[50]

Comedy Central's Stephen Colbert highlighted the moral callousness of the Heritage Foundation in a brilliant 2011 segment featuring Peter Edelman, the Associate Dean of Georgetown Law School who has battled on behalf of the poor for a half-century. If it takes satire to expose hypocritical tactics aimed at dismissing the dispossessed, we're all for it.[51]

The very idea of poverty being redefined by a think tank that caters to overpaid and under-taxed millionaires and billionaires should be nauseating. The only reason the Heritage report didn't elicit mass condemnation was because it reinforced stereotypes of cable-watching, XBox-playing, microwave-popcorn-eating government leeches.

It's no accident that the loudest voices that profit so handsomely from attacking the poor by denying the severity of their circumstances tend to be politicians, pundits, and think tanks aligned with and funded by corporate plutocrats and Wall Street oligarchs. America's elite understands that today's poor are a potential powerhouse. They are multicultural, multiracial, and multigenerational and come from a variety of backgrounds. There is no longer a one-size-fits-all poverty in America. If the 50 million poor ever reached consensus about the roots of their suffering, the plutocratic apple cart would be upended permanently.

This is why ignoring, denying, and dismissing the poor has become a multimillion-dollar enterprise.

Who's Boiling the Tea?

"The Founding Fathers originally said . . . they
put certain restrictions on who gets the right to vote.
It wasn't [that] you were just a citizen and you got to
vote. Some of the restrictions, you know, you obviously
would not think about today. But one of those was you
had to be a property owner."

Tea Party Nation President Judson Phillips was dead
serious in his attempt to justify the Founding Fathers'
decision of who should or shouldn't be allowed to vote
in this country: "And that makes a lot of sense, because
if you're a property owner, you actually have a vested
stake in the community. If you're not a property owner,
you know, I'm sorry but property owners have a little bit
more of a vested interest in the community than non-
property owners."[52]

On the surface it might seem odd that a leader of a
so-called populist movement would side with the elite.
However, when we peek behind the curtain, we see
who's spiking the tea and the motivations behind their
actions. *The New Yorker* and several other reputable media outlets have already exposed the ultra-conservative
moguls and ultra-rich foundations that fund Tea Party
candidates, campaigns, and propaganda. The party's
rebel yell against "big government," "wasteful spending," "Obamacare," and other sensationalized issues
has been scripted, packaged, and bankrolled by rich
moguls like the Koch Brothers and foundations such as
Freedom Works—an organization run by former GOP
Congressman Dick Armey and funded by the tobacco
giant Phillip Morris.[53]

Writing in the October 14, 2010, edition of *Rolling Stone* magazine, Matt Taibbi shared interesting insights about the Tea Party and the corporate insiders who created it. In the article, "The Truth about the Tea Party," Taibbi describes the audience gathered at a Kentucky Tea Party rally featuring former Alaska Governor Sarah Palin:

> "Scanning the thousands of hopped-up faces in the crowd, I am immediately struck by two things. One is that there isn't a single Black person here. The other is the truly awesome quantity of medical hardware: Seemingly every third person in the place is sucking oxygen from a tank or propping their giant atrophied glutes on motorized wheelchair-scooters."

Taibbi is told by a scooter-rider in the crowd why there were so many others in the auditorium: "The scooters are because of Medicare. . . . They have these commercials down here: 'You won't even have to pay for your scooter! Medicare will pay!' Practically everyone in Kentucky has one," the man said conspiratorially.

To confirm this disclosure, Taibbi talked to other "Medicare-motor-scooter conservatives" as they headed to the parking lot. He met an elderly couple, Janice and David Wheelock. David is an appraiser; Janice—who uses a scooter—is on Medicare. David, who claims to be "anti-spending and anti-government," complained that the "welfare state is out of control."

Incredulous, Taibbi asked the elderly man how he can rail against the welfare state when he had been collecting government checks for decades.

"Well," David answered, "there are a lot of people on welfare who don't deserve it. Too many people are living off the government."[54]

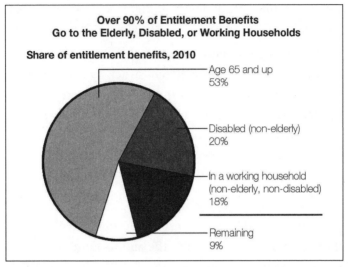

Over 90% of Entitlement Benefits Go to the Elderly, Disabled, or Working Households

Share of entitlement benefits, 2010

Age 65 and up
53%

Disabled (non-elderly)
20%

In a working household (non-elderly, non-disabled)
18%

Remaining
9%

Based on data from the U.S. Census Bureau, Office of Management and Budget, U.S. Departments of Agriculture, Health and Human Services, and Labor, and the Center on Budget and Policy Priorities.

The exchange speaks not only to the Tea Party mind-set but also that of a great number of Americans. They've been conditioned to separate themselves from "others" who need and use "big government" just like they do.

The brigade of Tea Party folk, in reality, consists of people who are simply distracted, aroused, angry, and vocal about government waste while the powerful puppet masters count their personal profits.

THE POVERTY DENIERS

At the time of this writing, the United States had experienced at least 3½ years of economic turmoil. During this period, more Americans than since the Great Depression have experienced unemployment, underemployment, and homelessness; and many are generally fearful about their financial future. Yet, most, including the fragile middle class, still ignore the poor and are defensively inclined to separate themselves from them. They have been misled to believe that America is really not a country of the "haves" and "have-nots."

A 2011 Rasmussen Report revealed that most Americans actually ascribe to the distorted Heritage Foundation view. The survey, based on government studies, found that 63 percent of American adults believe that people with a decent place to live, adequate food supplies, color televisions, and other amenities in the home are "not so poor."[55]

The findings show that little has changed in American attitudes relating to poverty since before the recession started in late 2007. In fact, the perception that America is not a country divided between the "haves" and "have-nots" has remained basically consistent over the past two decades.

A Gallup poll conducted November 28–December 1, 2011, found that 58 percent of Americans believe they fit in the "haves" category rather than the "have-nots" group. The survey also found that 58 percent of Democrats, 37 percent of Independents, and 26 percent of Republicans viewed the country as divided between the rich and poor—or the rich and the rest of us.[56]

In the recent past, it was Reagan who legitimized and sanctioned the attack on government helping the poor. Today, the Tea Party and right-wing pundits have positioned themselves behind the media-tized assault weapons. It's little wonder then that almost half of all Americans blame the government for poverty's increase. Another Fall 2011 Rasmussen Report revealed that 45 percent of Americans believe anti-poverty programs actually increased poverty in this country. Only 18 percent said the programs decreased poverty, while another 24 percent said government had no impact whatsoever.[57]

No matter the overwhelming evidence that American families, children, cities, and whole communities are sliding into abject poverty, many of our citizens hang on to the myth of American exceptionalism like a drowning man clinging to a concrete block. These sentiments allow the poor to be relatively absent from our public consciousness and barely marginal to our personal responsibility.

The Occupy Wall Street demonstrations openly challenged the American economic equation and the illusion of opportunity for all. By positioning the interest of America's struggling 99 percent against the obscene profits and rewards of its powerful 1 percent, the movement delivered a powerful and resonate message.

It's no accident that Fox News's Bill O'Reilly began our October 11, 2011, interview with him by suggesting that most impoverished Americans cannot and will not earn a decent living owing to substance dependency. Unbelievable. But Cornel and I literally jumped out of our chairs when O'Reilly then claimed that Wall Street bankers violated no laws in the financial meltdown that helped fuel one of the worst recessions in American history. Incredulously, he further depicted Occupy Wall Street protesters as socialists intent on having the government forcibly seize the assets of the wealthy and distribute them to the poor. Our smack-down of our dear brother was fair, but not balanced.[58]

The pundits, politicians, and fringe parties comfortably aligned with the wealthy 1 percent may soon have to check themselves. They can keep pretending this economic fiasco is all President Obama's fault if they want, but it might be at their own peril. It seems Americans across the board are starting to peek behind the curtain, and more and more are voicing displeasure about the rich wizards they behold.

In January 2012, the Pew Research Center released a poll that confirmed that "nearly two-thirds of Americans now believe the wealth gap is the greatest cause of tension in America."[59] This growing perception of the wealth gap is not the reflections of just minorities and Occupy Wall Street–type liberals. The biggest jump in class awareness was among white respondents. On the political spectrum, in 2009, only 38 percent of Republicans admitted there was a class conflict. The Pew report now puts that number at 55 percent.

> ". . . nearly two-thirds of Americans now believe the wealth gap is the greatest cause of tension in America. The number of whites who believe that there is a 'strong or very strong conflict between the rich and the poor' shot up from 43 percent in 2009 to 65 percent in just two years."

Does the poll mean that more whites and conservatives are going to don their khakis and bandanas and join the Occupy movement? No. Is it an indication of a massive voter turnout for Obama in 2012? Of course not.

It means that people are starting to recognize the divide and on which side they stand. It could mean that there's a chance to shatter the bipartisan consensus in Washington that poor people are not as important as the rest of us. Affirming that there is a distinctive and destructive rich/poor divide may convince folk like Brenda Caradine of Columbus, Mississippi, that we have a shared interest in the humanity of our fellow citizens. Like the beloved playwright Tennessee Williams, who taught us that we must not remain in a world of make-believe, Caradine and other fellow citizens must engage reality, history, and the possibility of change.

Who knows, it might make a poor Mississippi resident feel that he and his wife's blues are our blues, too. Hopefully, it will mean that they will no longer have to lyrically express their personal catastrophe alone.

CHAPTER 4

Poverty of Courage

"The future does not belong to those who are content with today, apathetic toward common problems and their fellow man alike. Rather it will belong to those who can blend vision, reason, and courage in a personal commitment to the ideals and great enterprises of American society."

—Robert Kennedy, 1968

"I say housing is a human right!"
"That's why we stand and fight!"
"Again, housing is a human right!"
"That's why we stand and fight!"

The call-and-response chanting came from a coalition of grassroots agencies operating under the banner "Take Back the Land, Madison." The Wisconsin activists, who believe housing is a human right, seize and occupy abandoned homes for homeless families *without consent*.

For years, consumer advocates, human-rights and political activists, and others have called on the Obama administration to aggressively investigate and prosecute bankers and lenders whose actions led to the worst housing crisis in decades. We now know that the housing and subprime mortgage bonanza was rife with fraud and deception. This complicated enterprise included bankers, appraisers, notaries, investors, and disreputable middlemen who fabricated, altered, and cobbled suspect documentation together to sell properties quickly— whether people could afford them or not. Yet, despite these criminal manipulations, far too few of these elite suspects have been investigated or prosecuted.

The disenfranchised aren't waiting for justice from the government. In cities like New York, Chicago, Los Angeles, New Orleans, Minneapolis, and Boston, grass-roots and activist agencies and everyday people (including the homeless) are staging Occupy Wall Street–type efforts to reclaim abandoned or foreclosed properties.

Our poverty tour bus pulled up to a foreclosed, brick duplex on Hammersley Road in Madison. Lavender leaflets pasted on the residence's window warned trespassers of arrests and possible fines. The notices did not seem to deter the diverse group we observed. Their actions, though illegal, they say are highly moral.

"So the reason we are talking about housing in a material sense is because that's simply how you have to talk about it in a capitalistic society," Monica, a Take Back the Land activist, told us. "There's no other way to talk about it unless I say 'I own this house.'"

We challenged their assertions, asking how they'd respond to people who consider their actions illegal and immoral. Members who had been evicted from that particular duplex and other area homes due to foreclosures described the campaign as "positive action" designed to break "immoral laws which allow banks to gain billions in profits while human beings are made homeless."

We witnessed similar acts of resistance on other poverty tour stops. In Chicago we toured the public housing complex where Dr. King and his family once lived. According to the Chicago Coalition for the Homeless, there are 65,184 people on the public-housing waiting list in the city of Chicago alone—more than the total available public-housing units (63,810) in the entire state of Illinois. Meanwhile, entire blocks of boarded-up and abandoned buildings dominate the Windy City's landscape.

We interviewed Willie "J. R." Fleming, co-founder of the Chicago Anti-Eviction Campaign. Not only does the agency place families in vacant foreclosed homes, they also involve the community, asking neighbors surrounding the home to sign pledges to block court-ordered police evictions.

While sitting on the concrete steps of one of those "occupied" dwellings, Fleming defined the rationale behind the group's radical approach:

> "Our anti-eviction campaign was born because people from different parts of the city—the Black community, white community, and Latino community—saw that their housing was leaving. Our struggle is related to education, labor, and housing cuts—all of these struggles are intertwined."

Unoccupied, blighted, and foreclosed properties are "health hazards" to the community, Fleming said. Since no one's forcing the banks to come to the table and discuss rates that poor and struggling people can afford, "the people of the community are house sitting or community sitting." It's called the "community economic development plan," Fleming added.

The housing crisis has endangered the American Dream—where every family can own a home or simply have a decent place to live and raise their families. Say what you will about the home occupiers' tactics, they have the courage to speak truth to power—and they refuse to be powerless. They have the audacity and courage to take on a multibillion-dollar institution.

Their strategies may be illegal, but so were the protests that preceded the American Revolution and many of the sit-ins and demonstrations that personified the civil-rights and women's-rights movements. An unmistakable theme sparks and circulates throughout these movements. When the rich exploit the poor, the working poor, or the newly poor, there will be moral outrage, and American history teaches us that there will be resistance.

THE AFFLUENCE OF THE FEW

"Whenever there is great prosperity, there is great inequality. For one very rich man, there must be at least five hundred poor, and the affluence of the few supposes the indigence of the many."
—Adam Smith

The 13 colonies that made up what was to become the United States were determined to break from the tyranny of the British monarchy. Early Americans rejected Europe's aristocratic rule and opted instead for a government based on "republicanism"—a system where elected officials were to be responsive to the will of the people. Europe was forced to concede its territory after a bloody eight-year war that seeded democracy and formed a core set of values that would continue to challenge and shape economic, political, and social life in America for centuries to come.

What's missing in most American history books is the extent to which this country amassed its riches from free, Black slave labor. In his book, *A People's History of the United States, 1492–Present* (New York: Harper, 2003), professor, activist, and author Howard Zinn defines the cruelty of human bondage aggravated by "the frenzy for limitless profit that comes from capitalistic agriculture."[60]

Academy Award–winning filmmaker, best-selling author, and social critic Michael Moore elaborated on this theme during the "Remaking America" symposium:

> "This is a nation founded on genocide and built on the backs of slaves," Moore said. "We tried to actually eliminate one entire race. Then we used another race to build this country, actually quite quickly as a new country, into a world power. This country never would have had the wealth that it had, had it not had slavery for a couple of hundred years."

Moore speaks truth. The accumulation of capital derived from agricultural products such as tobacco, cotton, and rice produced by slaves provided funds needed for research and perfecting the new technologies that fueled the rapid pace of American industrialization.[61]

America's Industrial Age created some of its first millionaires. During this time the U.S. economy grew at the fastest rate in its history, with real wages, wealth, gross domestic product (GDP), and capital formation increasing at unprecedented rates. Capitalism in the 19th century flourished under the government's laissez-faire ("leave it alone") policy pioneered by 18th-century capitalist Adam Smith. It was a time when steel, finance, oil, industrial consolidation, and transportation by rail and sea stamped names like Andrew Carnegie, Andrew W. Mellon, J. P. Morgan, John D. Rockefeller, and Charles M. Schwab into America's consciousness.[62]

The advent of the steam engine, for example, changed a world that delivered raw materials by horse-drawn wagons to one where freight was shipped by steamships and locomotives. But, along with improved standards of living and advanced systems of transportation, communication, banking, machinery, and mass production came an era of gross exploitation of men, women, and children. At the height of the Industrial Revolution, the average American worked 12-hour days and seven-day weeks just to eke out a basic living. Children as young as five or six toiled in mills, factories, and mines, earning a fraction of the measly wages adults were paid at the time.[63]

Inspired by the notion of Republicanism, advocates for the poor drew sharp public focus to the divide
between America's rich and very poor. In his critique
of upper-class opulence, Mark Twain coined the phrase
"Gilded Age" to define such affluence in the late 19th
century.[64]

Critics wrote commentaries, gave speeches, and
convened public meetings that challenged and mocked
the massively rich capitalists. The Carnegies, Rockefell-
ers, and other mega-rich industrialists and financiers
were caricatured as "robber barons"—pompous, musta-
chioed men in black top hats, coats, and tails. In fact,
Rich Uncle Pennybags, the mascot for the popular board
game *Monopoly*, is based on the robber baron caricature.

By 1886, stronger and more organized labor unions
such as the Knights of Labor—rooted in common
working-class values—demanded higher wages, shorter
hours, safer working conditions, and bargaining rights
for the working man. These were not exactly peaceful
pleas. Among industrialized nations, the United States
has one of the bloodiest histories of labor battles. The
Great Railroad Strike of 1877, for example, which lasted
45 days, had become so violent that President Ruth-
erford B. Hayes had no choice but to send in federal
troops to quell attacks against railroad property and
personnel.

The heavy-handed police tactics seen during the
Occupy Wall Street protests are mild in comparison to
skirmishes between laborers and authorities intent on
protecting the interests of wealthy business owners and

employers. State police were called out nearly 500 times between 1875 and 1910 to quell labor unrest. The annual May Day celebration—a holiday most acknowledge with parades, beer, and barbecue—is really a commemoration of the achievements of common workers, labor organizations, and the thousands who lost their lives during hundreds of bloody confrontations for workers' rights.

Economic exploitation re-ignited the long struggles of women, emancipated slaves, and Native Americans. It sparked the anger of immigrants who arrived on these shores only to realize that they were little more than human machines harnessed to fuel the profit objectives of powerful industrialists.

By the dawn of the 20th century, a multifaceted social unrest had intensified in America. Women, Blacks, and Latinos championed separate issues, but a binding cause stretching back to the genesis of America empowered the dispossessed to speak up and take collective action. Throughout the abolitionist, women's-suffrage, and civil-rights movements; and the Mexican American workers'-rights strikes first led by activist César Chávez, one phrase served as the indisputable and powerful rallying cry: "Economic Justice!"

THE NEW CIVIL RIGHTS BATTLE

"Courage is what it takes to stand up and speak; courage is also what it takes to sit down and listen."
—Winston Churchill

The fight for fairness has deep roots in America's great struggles for justice and equality. The issue of poverty, like slavery and the oppression of women, was considered by most to be the natural order of things. The poor face the same dilemmas as oppressed Blacks and women whose fates were tolerated, legitimized, and rationalized because wealthy, dominant forces needed a permanent underclass to maintain their lavish lifestyles.

The connections between the abolitionists' and women's-rights movements to today's poverty and the ever-widening gap between the rich and the poor are evident. Iconic figures from bygone eras such as Frederick Douglass and Elizabeth Cady Stanton could easily be today's voices for poor people with a simple substitution of key words:

Douglass:

"The white man's happiness cannot be purchased by the Black man's misery."

The rich man's happiness cannot be purchased by **the poor** man's misery.

Stanton:

"So long as women are slaves, men will be knaves."

So long as **the poor** are slaves, **the rich** will be knaves.

Poverty is 21st-century-style slavery; its eradication should serve as the battle cry of a new civil rights movement. Although most Americans remember and celebrate Dr. Martin Luther King's commitment to nonviolent social change, the cause that consumed his final days was the elimination of poverty. In the article, "King's Final Message: Poverty is a civil rights battle," journalist Stephanie Siek explored this topic with people and experts who are familiar with King's legacy.

According to accounts retold by his intimates, Dr. King spent his last birthday, January 15, 1968, working on "The Poor People's Campaign"—a planned demonstration in Washington, DC. It was designed to bring the issue of poverty among "all races, religions, and backgrounds" to the forefront of America's consciousness and conscience.

"At the time of his death," Siek wrote, "King was pushing an idea that might be considered among his most radical: Not only should poverty be eradicated, he argued, but everyone should be guaranteed an income that would prevent them from falling into poverty."[65]

King's words from a speech delivered in Grosse Pointe, Michigan, less than a month before his assassination, emphasized this point:

> "The problem of unemployment is not the only problem. There is a problem of underemployment. . . . Most of the poverty-stricken people of America are persons who are working every day, and they end up getting part-time wages for full-time work."

Dr. King once said: "Our lives begin to end the day we become silent about things that matter." The day he was assassinated, he was in Memphis, Tennessee, to speak out against the horrendous working conditions and poverty-level wages endured by 1,300 striking sanitation workers.

No matter how formidable their power, influence, or prestige, King summoned the courage to confront those who enabled poverty and economic injustice. Because it mattered.

WAR—THE ENEMY OF THE POOR

"Faced with what is right, to leave it undone shows a lack of courage."
—Confucius

In his speech, "Beyond Vietnam: A Time to Break Silence," Dr. King spoke of "a shining moment" when he felt the nation's fledgling poverty programs held promise and "hope for the poor—both Black and white."

Then, King said, came the buildup in Vietnam:

"I watched this program broken and eviscerated, as if it was some idle political plaything of a society gone mad on war, and I knew that America would never invest the necessary funds or energies in rehabilitation of its poor so long as adventures like Vietnam continued to draw men and skills and money like some demonic destructive suction tube."[66]

Anytime you seriously dissect the issue of poverty, you have to talk about wealth and income inequality. A productive discussion about poverty must lead to common-sense conversations about wise investments in education, housing, health care, job training, and other efforts that increase poor people's access to resources of all kinds. We have no choice but to talk about the military industrial complex and its ties to huge private-sector monopolies and war barons who produce weaponry and employ privatized security personnel at salaries that far exceed what we pay government military personnel for the same services.'

We think most Americans now agree with us that the more than a trillion dollars (and counting) it has cost the American taxpayer to execute and maintain our military adventures in Afghanistan and Iraq was a monumental mistake. When George W. Bush entered office in 2001, he inherited a healthy budget surplus left by his predecessor, Bill Clinton. It wasn't welfare, housing vouchers, or Medicaid that wiped out this surplus and pushed the country into the Great Recession. As Teresa Tritch wrote in her *New York Times* article, "How the Deficit Got This Big" (July 23, 2011), the primary factors that led to our current deficit dilemma were war spending and Bush-era tax cuts for the rich.[67]

According to researchers at Brown University's Watson Institute for International Studies, 225,000 lives have been lost in the Afghanistan and Iraq wars; these wars will eventually cost Americans between $3.2 and $4 trillion. By comparison, the Vietnam War cost $686 billion. The wars in Iraq and Afghanistan are the second-most expensive military conflicts in American history, behind World War II, which cost—in inflation-adjusted dollars—$4.1 trillion, according to a 2008

Congressional Research Service study.[68]

In its June 2011 report, "The Cost of War," the Brown University research center noted how America used to pay for wars by elevating the tax rate and/or by selling war bonds. The study stressed how the current wars "were paid for almost entirely by borrowing that raised the deficit and increased the national debt."[69]

What good could we have accomplished in our own nation with a trillion-dollar infusion? Several agencies and news organizations have done the math. Following is just a sample of the social progress we could have made with just $1 trillion of the money invested in these wars since 2003.

Researchers at Brown University's Watson Institute for International Studies calculated what $1.3 trillion of war spending by the Department of Defense could have looked like if spent to create jobs in the private sector over the past decade. The amount broken down annually comes to $130 billion. With that amount the United States could have created 1.3 trillion dollars' worth of jobs.

Jobs in Education	936,000
Jobs in Healthcare	780,000
Jobs in Construction	364,000
Jobs in Renewable Energy (solar, wind, or biomass etc.)	52,000

How many young people could we have helped enroll in college with just a fraction of that $1 trillion? Surely the gap between the very rich and very poor would narrow if more of our young people were given the support necessary to attend community and four-year colleges. Such institutions are where they can gain the skills necessary to compete in the global market-place. Ironically, if students had access to interest-free loans like big banks do, many young people would flourish with less debt.

The United Faculty of Washington State (UFWS), an educational collective dedicated to promoting and defending the funding of public universities, addressed this issue directly. "Now more than ever, poor people fight rich people's wars," a 2009 UFWS commentary de-clared. The article outlined the history and ramifications of government disinvestment in public universities:

> "Since the 1980s, states have been steadily disin-vesting in public universities and replacing state appropriations with increased tuition. So as the military has become more and more the place where the dispossessed go for some economic stability, state universities have become more and more the playgrounds of the privileged."[70]

Perhaps more young people could have received a little "economic stability" if not for the billions show-ered upon private military firms and wasted in Iraq.

The "Cost of War" report also spoke to the boondog-gle private companies reaped from military expeditions. Halliburton, for example—the energy company once led by former Vice President Dick Cheney—saw its contracts swell from "$483 million in 2002 to over $6 billion in 2006," which included controversial no-bid contracts awarded even before the Iraq invasion in 2003.

Where were the cries of "irresponsible government" after tens of billions of dollars—quietly shipped from the New York Federal Reserve to the Central Bank of Iraq—went missing? Between 2003 and 2008, after the fall of Saddam Hussein, reportedly much of the $40 billion in cash sent to Iraq for the reconstruction and restructuring of government services was stolen, misappropriated, or mysteriously lost.[71]

It is because of these travesties that the 2011 deficit-reduction debate and the fallout over increasing the nation's debt ceiling—which left Congress in a state of paralysis for months—were such shams. House Speaker John Boehner's $1.2 trillion deficit-reduction plan included no cuts in Afghanistan and Iraq war spending but drastic cuts to Social Security, Medicare, Medicaid, and other programs that help the economically vulnerable and desperately poor.

As progressive Senator Bernie Sanders (I-Vt.) argued in a blistering July 2011 *Wall Street Journal* editorial, the plan offered by Democrats rendered almost as much harm to the poor as Boehner's proposal:

> "The plan by Senate Majority Leader Harry Reid, which calls for $2.4 trillion in cuts over a 10-year period, includes $900 billion in cuts in areas such as education, health care, nutrition, affordable housing, child care, and many other programs desperately needed by working families and the most vulnerable."

In short, there are always those who profit from war,

but the poor pay the price. An African proverb states that when elephants fight, it's the ground that suffers. So too, when countries are at war, everyday people are the ones who get trampled.

So, Dr. King was right: "War is the enemy of the poor."

THE AUDACITY OF COURAGE

On a hot summer day in August 2011, we parked our bus in an abandoned shopping mall parking lot just outside of Ann Arbor, Michigan, and headed out on foot. We gingerly traipsed along the hazardous shoulder of the two-lane Highway 94, over a bridge, to an opening not visible to speeding passersby. We were led down steps fashioned out of dried mud. About 100 meters or so through a thickly wooded area, we came to an opening littered with camping equipment, ice chests, and tents of all colors and sizes.

Welcome to Camp Take Notice, a place that holds roughly 50 people (ages 45 to 65, we were told) with no other place to call home. At the time of our visit, this was the fifth location where they had set up camp. Campers had been evicted from other locations by the state department of transportation.

At the camp, we were introduced to Jackie Starkey, a grandmotherly woman with a thin body and thinning blonde hair. Stress and worry accentuated the words she used to convey the story of her life in the woods. Starkey found herself with no money and no home during the Great Recession. She stayed with family members for a brief period, but that option was exhausted, she said—with little detail. She went to homeless shelters in Ann Arbor, but due to overcrowding, there "was no room at the inn," she joked sadly. In fact, it was someone from one of the shelters who suggested she go to the tent city.

"It really gets frustrating," Starkey told us. "It's like, why couldn't they help me? Why did I have to be homeless to get any help?"

A younger-looking couple stood nearby, listening intently as Starkey talked to us. A worried look creased the woman's face. Was she empathizing with Starkey or thinking about her own situation? She stood silently—arms crossed, shifting from foot to foot. The young man—bald, with a tuft of hair on his chin shaped like an exclamation point—stared at the ground. One of his hands held a cup; the other rubbed the worried woman's shoulder.

The couple didn't accept our invitation to share their stories. Who could blame them? Not everyone is willing to admit they've hit rock bottom on national television. At the time of this writing, about 680,00 people were experiencing homelessness on any given night in the United States, according to the National Alliance to End Homelessness. There is no reason to believe that number has been reduced by any significant amount since.[72]

The eradication of poverty is a cause that is in desperate need of truth-tellers. If no one honestly speaks out about the suffering of the dispossessed, their pain will never be heard. Put another way, a condition of truth is to allow the suffering to speak. We can't get to truth if the voices of the poor remain muted. Whites led the abolitionist movement, but it took a former slave by the name of Frederick Douglass to give the cause authenticity. White men were involved with the women's-suffrage movement, but social activist Elizabeth Cady Stanton represented the urgency of the battle for women's rights.

Great social change requires persons who possess the courage to tell the truth, to fight for justice, and to be so committed to that truth that they are willing to risk death. No small matter.

The voiceless are in desperate need of resolute and committed voices.

A MATTER OF COURAGE

"In this nation I see tens of millions of its citizens
—a substantial part of its whole population—
who at this very moment are denied the greater part
of what the very lowest standards of today
call the necessities of life."

—FDR

In his second inaugural address delivered January 20, 1937, President Franklin D. Roosevelt asked the nation to rise to the challenge of unemployment and poverty in America. With bold exhortation, FDR spoke for the millions of Americans he saw who were "trying to live on incomes so meager that the pall of family disaster hangs over them day by day." FDR spoke on behalf of those living in cities and on farms under conditions labeled indecent by "a so-called polite society . . ." His speech showed profound compassion for children denied education and recreation, and parents denied the opportunity to better their lot in life and that of their children. As he confirmed that one-third of the nation was "ill-housed, ill-clad, and ill-nourished," Roosevelt declared that poverty denies "work and productiveness."

The point, he maintained, was not to paint a picture of despair but to inspire the nation to face and rise above the "superfluous" borders that keep the divide between the rich and the poor so expansive: "The test of our progress is not whether we add more to the abundance of those who have much; it is whether we provide enough for those who have too little," he said.

FDR's decision to take the nation far beyond the comfort zone of exceptionalism is an example of the unyielding and uncompromising courage needed to arrest the scourge of poverty today. What's missing in today's political arena are bold advocates for the poor who will risk careers, stature, and political office to be their brothers' and sisters' keepers. Also absent is the courage to stand against powerful multinational corporations, Wall Street elites, and a socio-political system that blindly favors the rich and the lucky over everyday people.

Now, to be sure, most politicians campaigning for the 2012 election—from town councils to the White House—will offer perfectly phrased sound bites about the need to help the middle class. It's the safest territory. The majority of the sliding middle class and the new poor are white voters. Supporting the middle class has no inherent risks; it demands no special sacrifice.

"Employing the poor and eradicating poverty" is verbiage that has not been heard in the White House since President Lyndon Johnson occupied the Oval Office.

Fear is the underlying radioactive element that suppresses the truth about poverty. When we get serious about eradicating poverty, we become trespassers, crossing over onto the invisibly gated property of those who have profited from America's wealth at the expense of America's unfortunate. This is terrifying terrain for most politicians.

Why? Because it takes millions of dollars to become the President of the United States, a member of Congress, a governor, a state legislator, and sometimes even a mayor. President Obama raised nearly $750 million for his 2008 presidential campaign. His Republican opponent, Arizona Senator John McCain, raised almost $300 million. Presidential campaigns are heavily dependent on campaign contributions from the filthy rich and the lobbyists who represent multinational corporations and fat-cat Wall Street firms.

Many regard lobbying as it is practiced today as little more than legalized bribery built on normalized corruption. Indeed, some elected officials manage against the odds to maintain their *"Mr. Smith Goes to Washington"* passion and purity. But too often, once lobbyists begin to exert their extraordinary influence, previously principled men and women sometimes become pawns in a game that only the spineless survive.

This is why there has been such an absence of serious investigation into the housing crisis and no indictments against the multibillionaire bankers who profited from the subprime lending boom. In his 2012 State of the Union address, President Obama said that he plans to create a federal mortgage crisis unit charged with investigating the alleged wrongdoings of bankers related to real estate lending. That's all fine and good. However, just weeks after this announcement, the administration revealed it had reached a $25 billion settlement deal with bankers. We can only hope that this deal doesn't omit the criminal investigations. After all, that's how it works in the world of the rich and infamous. A poor man would be sent directly to jail if he were caught hustling innocents. But on today's *Monopoly* board of life, the Rich Uncle Pennybags on Wall Street—accused of hustling millions—are given billions in bailout money that they can hoard, invest, and very well turn around and use to pay off a "settlement" in lieu of jail time.

Fear prohibits politicians from voicing these types of costly truths. Putting on the armor to join the fight against poverty demands that we confront our own fear—fear that allows us to remain silent or downplay the truth and tolerate lies; fear of losing campaign funds, an election, or popularity; or fear of retaliation or other unknown consequences. Courage is not the absence of fear, but rather the capacity to stand in one's truth with integrity no matter the consequences.

The lives of Harriet Tubman, President Abraham Lincoln, civil rights advocate Medgar Evers, Unitarian minister Rev. James Reeb, housewife and mother Viola Gregg Liuzzo, Dr. King, Fannie Lou Hamer, and many, many others all ended in pursuit of convictions they believed were well worth the ultimate sacrifice.

For Dr. King's Christian calling that compelled him to "see the war as an enemy of the poor and to attack it as such," he was denounced, defamed, and widely dethroned as a legitimate voice for America's dispossessed.[73] It took tremendous courage to endure the character assassinations by President Lyndon Johnson, other politicians, mainstream media, the public at large, and even those in his intimate Black leadership circles. Nevertheless, Dr. King was determined to tell the truth, fight for justice, and risk death. He died embodying his love for poor people.

In our time, especially now that the Iraq war is over, can our nation rise to Roosevelt's 1937 challenge—to seek progress that doesn't cater to those who have too much and provides for "those who have too little?" Will we have the King-like courage to demand that our government invest wisely to enable and ennoble the one out of two Americans who are presently in or near poverty? The future of American democracy rests on how we answer this critical question.

CHAPTER 5

Poverty of Compassion

"Compassion constitutes a radical form of criticism, for it announces that the hurt is to be taken seriously, that the hurt is not to be accepted as normal and natural, but it is an abnormal and unacceptable condition for humanness. Thus compassion that might be seen simply as generous goodwill is in fact criticism of the system, forces, and ideologies that produce the hurt."

—Walter Brueggemann

"What is it like to be the head of the United States Department of Education when you live in a nation where the value of a poor child's life is less than that of a rich child's life?"

Secretary Arne Duncan seemed a bit taken aback by the question asked in late 2011, when Cornel met with the Secretary at his Washington office. They discussed the government's $4 billion "Race to the Top" competition and other matters related to education and the poor.

Cornel's query is more than justified by government

statistics. We do not believe the Black/white achieve-ment gap captures the complexity of the education crisis in America. Although there have been modest gains in reducing this gap, Black children still score lower on mathematics and reading tests than whites. And more than 50 percent of Black children drop out of high school as compared to 30 percent of students overall. We know that these statistics do not just reflect the edu-cational barriers; they also reflect the insidious nature of poverty as it ruptures the lives of our children.[74]

According to the National Poverty Center, children make up 36 percent of the nation's poor. Black children comprise 38.2 percent of that number, while Hispanics make up 35.0 percent and white children are 12.4 per-cent.[75] Poverty is linked to an array of related problems that feed the achievement gap like low birthweight, exposure to lead poisoning, hunger, neglect, frequent school-changing, underfunded schools, and less paren-tal involvement. Is this the way that it has to be in the richest nation in the world?

Finland's students are ranked number one in the world in science and math. Over 90 percent of Finnish teachers are unionized, and the top graduates of Fin-land's universities become teachers rather than invest-ment bankers. The sons and daughters of America's moneyed elite perform at levels comparable to Finland's students. However, when poverty enters the picture, too often American students fall prey to an irreversible downward spiral of poor performance.

In the meeting with Cornel, Duncan argued that the Obama administration has made closing the educational achievement gap in America a top priority, and that the Race to the Top educational program serves as a sign of that commitment.

Cornel was blunt in his retort:

"I know you all are break dancing over this $4 billion initiative, but Afghanistan gets $4 billion every day. So, militarism trumps any case of poverty and poor children. That's the country's priorities and how warped our priorities are!"

It's hard to deny that there is an indefensible poverty of compassion for America's poor children. As a collective, we've failed to demonstrate the concern, the care required to make certain that they are properly cherished and nurtured. If Americans cultivated a surplus of compassion, our children would not be without food, shelter, and quality health care. If we really cherished our babies, we'd dedicate more resources to schools that will churn out fewer soldiers and more doctors, teachers, engineers, and scientists. With a surplus of love, the untapped potential of our youth would not rot away in our nation's prisons.

Are Americans just mouthing a cliché when they say "the children are our future"? Or perhaps Americans aren't talking about *all* of our children. Maybe, in America, we've resigned ourselves to the fact that only those who live in the right zip codes deserve a quality education. If so, we are destined for a dismal future.

Every year, an estimated 1.3 million American students drop out of high school, and most of those are poor children of color. Roughly 68 percent of 12th graders who attend "high-poverty schools" graduate while 91 percent from "low-poverty schools" earn their diplomas.[76] Without serious intervention, 13 million students will drop out within the next 10 years at a cost of more than $3 trillion in earning potential for the nation, according to the Alliance for Excellent Education.

No matter how we protest, these statistics indicate how disconnected we are and how little we value children, especially poor children of color. Therefore the question posed to the Secretary must be rephrased: "What's it like to be part of a country, known for its prosperity, where the value of a poor child's life is less than the value of an affluent child's life?"

"YOU GOTTA SACRIFICE FOR YOUR CHILD"

"At the end of the day, love and compassion will win."
—Former hostage and humanitarian Terry Waite

Joseph, a blue-collar Italian American, grew up on Long Island, New York. For most of his adult life, he worked in auto body shops painting cars. Joseph and his wife never made a lot of money, but with her salary as a bookkeeper, the couple was able to buy a split-level home in Medford, Suffolk County, about 11 years ago. They have a son, Joey. Life was good. But that was then.

"I am totally broke. I live paycheck to paycheck. I can't pay all the bills. I don't qualify for anything."

Joseph's story, part of the CDF's "'Held Captive': Child Poverty in America" report, caught our attention because he's one of the nearly 21 percent of single dads in this country living in poverty, according to the 2010 U.S. Census data. The 41 percent poverty rate for single moms with children under the age of 18 is much higher; the percentage for both single moms and dads is still higher than that of impoverished married couples with children at 9 percent.[76]

Joseph's wife has multiple sclerosis. Her condition has deteriorated to the point where Joseph had no choice but to put her in a nursing home. With the loss of the second income, Joseph joined the ranks of the working poor. At the time of his interview with Cass, Joseph had been laid off twice in the past few years but found another job that barely pays enough for him and his son, a strapping 16-year-old at the time, to get by. As a result, he has had to turn to area food banks.

"It's not easy being a single fella," Joseph said, explaining how his number-one priority is caring for his son. "I try to shield him. I've been taking all the sacrifices. . . . I try to shield him to the best of my ability except for the grief over his mom. Nobody has control over that. She's just hanging in there."

Joseph, who is among the 49.9 million Americans without health insurance,[77] is concerned about his own health:

> "I'm worried because I wake up snoring. I think I might have sleep apnea. I could go to a clinic, but I need a specialist, so I'm just letting that go. I can't take off work anyway. You take a day off and they really need you, they get someone to replace you."

Joseph said he's barely hanging on, "just taking it

day by day and week by week," doing what it takes to raise his son:

> "I've learned to eat a little something in the morning. I don't eat lunch. I drink from the hose at work. That's just how things are. You gotta sacrifice for your child."

Joseph's "sacrifice" is one that no impoverished parent in America should have to make.

TO BE FULLY HUMAN

> *"Compassion automatically invites you to relate with people because you no longer regard people as a drain on your energy."*
> —Chogyam Trungpa

As we've illustrated in previous chapters, over the centuries there has been an ebb and flow of compassion for the poor in America. Political leadership, strong advocacy, and good and bad economic times all impact our collective concern for our fellow man. In these modern, digitized, survival-of-the-fittest times, we've become colder and increasingly distant. The phrase "I am my brother's keeper" has become passé. We place individual over community. We judge first and ask questions later. It's not that the system is unjust and inhumane; too many of us believe that there's something innately wrong with the poor.

When it comes to genuine compassion for the poor, a country that takes pride in its so-called Christian values has somehow lost its way.

JUSTICE FOR ALL, SERVICE TO OTHERS, AND A LOVE THAT LIBERATES

"All major religious traditions carry basically the same message; that is love, compassion, and forgiveness. The important thing is they should be part of our daily lives."

—Dalai Lama

Walter Rauschenbusch—theologian, Baptist minister, key figure in the Social Gospel movement, and major influence on the life of Dr. Martin Luther King, Jr.—dedicated his life to the practice of a prophetic Christian theology that could change American society. He believed, quite simply, that a just society should reflect moral values and promote "justice for all, service to others, and a love that liberates."

Rauschenbusch lived and preached a gospel with no religious restrictions. Tenets of social justice can be found in the Catholic, Methodist, Jewish, Islamic, Hindu, and other faiths. It is the holistic idea that equality and solidarity should serve as the fundamental core of societies, institutions, communities, and lifestyles. Social justice emphasizes the value of human rights and recognizes the dignity of every human being.

Jesus Christ was the world's most famous social-justice activist. He was crucified by the Roman Empire because he ran the money changers out of the temple in Jerusalem. One key component of "Catholic social-justice teaching" is that "Human life must be valued above all material possessions." The United Methodist Church's *Book of Discipline* says, "It is a governmental responsibility to provide all citizens with health care."

In *To Heal a Fractured World: The Ethics of Responsibility* (New York: Random House, 2005), Rabbi Jonathan Sacks declares that social justice has a central place in Judaism. One of Judaism's "ethics of responsibility" is the concept of *chesed* ("deeds of kindness").

Social justice is woven into the history of social work, health care, human rights education, the Global Justice Movement, and numerous grassroots organizations, including The Green Party.

"A love that liberates" is more than a touchy-feely aspiration. It is the premise of Liberation Theology—a "bottom-up" movement based on Jesus's example to fight for the poor against unjust economic, political, or social conditions. This international and interdenominational movement uses social justice as its guide to provide hope and alleviate the poor's suffering and struggle.

Corporate capitalism tends to clash with this kind of social justice. It reduces human life to market calculation and co-modification. To be fully human, we cannot allow men, women, and children to live in poverty amid unprecedented prosperity.

This manifesto is founded on the fundamental conviction that there must be a renaissance of compassion in America: There can be no genuine compassion without a resurrection of an explosively radical movement of righteous indignation directed at eradicating poverty.

A RADICALLY DEMOCRATIC REVOLUTION

*"I am not interested in picking up crumbs of compassion
thrown from the table of someone who considers himself
my master. I want the full menu of rights."*

—Desmond Tutu

One of the most compelling historical examples in
American history of wedding righteous indignation to
democratic expansion is the Black prophetic tradition.
By this we mean the universal commitment to the dignity and sanctity of persons—beginning with the "least
of these"—and the commitment to live and die in the
struggle for freedom and democracy.

The Black prophetic tradition is the leaven in the
American democratic loaf. In its gallant struggles against
slavery in America, Jim Crow, and white supremacy,
this tradition enacted love and justice, not bigotry and
revenge. From this tradition came Harriet Tubman, Frederick Douglass, Ida B. Wells-Barnett, Martin Luther King,
Jr., and Fannie Lou Hamer, among others. The future of
American democracy depends on revitalizing the best
of this tradition now. The war to eradicate poverty is a
direct extension of this grand tradition.

When Americans are starving, there is a need for
revolution. Vicki B. Escarra, President and CEO of Feeding America, the nation's leading domestic hunger-relief
charity, talked about this "crisis" of compassion during
the "Remaking America" symposium:

"The numbers are huge. There are 50 million
Americans in this country that are hungry. That
means that they don't know where their next

meal is going to come from. If they are parents, they are fretting and worrying about how they're going to feed their children. If they are little kids, they're at school and they come in oftentimes on Monday mornings with not enough to eat; they're fidgety and not learning in classrooms. There are senior citizens that are living on a fixed income and they are too modest and embarrassed to ask for help."

Feeding America has been recognized for its outstanding research and programs on hunger in America. The numbers of poor people going to food banks and into food stamp offices for the first time has grown by 30 percent, Escarra said, adding:

"That 30 percent are people visiting that have never been there, so it is the middle class. We've seen the numbers, since the recession, doubled. Come on, guys, this is a crisis. We've got a crisis in front of us."

When people are starving, when people have no hope, democracy is threatened. An external threat is not our major concern. It's the internal rot that's ominously heading the country toward the point of no return. A dynamite fuse has been lit outside of the communities where the "safe class" resides in luxurious, gated spaces while working people and poor people are struggling in the bankruptcy of the streets.

Within the bosom of the Black prophetic tradition, liberation theology, and social justice advocacy, righteous indignation toward poverty is now given moral license to explode. These traditions demand that we reject violence but welcome public outrage at corporate and societal greed. As the poet Ralph Waldo Emerson reminds, "A good indignation brings out all one's powers." We are steadfast in our belief that the legacy of social justice remains the last hope for American democracy.

PRISONS AND THE POOR

> *". . . For I was hungry and you gave me food,*
> *I was thirsty and you gave me something to drink,*
> *I was a stranger and you welcomed me,*
> *I was naked and you gave me clothing,*
> *I was sick and you took care of me,*
> *I was in prison and you visited me."*
> —Matthew 25:34–36

Under the glaring beam of social justice, we see how this society has prostituted the theological interpretation of compassion. What does the conservative's claim on "family values" really mean when poor children are allowed to suffer? How can we take comfort in the phrase "one nation under God" when we ignore the examples of compassion dictated by Christ?

There is something warped about a society that has invested $300 billion for the expansion of the prison industrial complex's jails, prisons, and juvenile justice institutions while claiming it has no money for schools, housing the homeless, feeding the poor, or creating jobs with a living wage.

Yes, we hear the push-back, especially from the far-right corners about "personal responsibility," "family values," and how the breakdown of the family has actually contributed to generational poverty.

To be sure, we recognize that weak family structures often contribute to generations of poverty, but we also recognize that weak families are deeply shaped and molded by larger social, economic, and historical forces. You can't put out a fire with gasoline. You can't rectify an injustice with more injustices.

As Michelle Alexander brilliantly illustrates in her award-winning work, *The New Jim Crow: Mass Incarceration in the Age of Colorblindness,* a new racial caste and control system was designed as the criminal justice system after the elimination of America's Jim Crow laws. The number of people behind bars has grown from 300,000 in the 1970s to more than 2.5 million today, and almost half—846,000, or 40.2 percent—of the prison occupiers are African American. As Alexander notes, there are more African American adults under correctional control today—either in prisons or jails, on probation, or on parole—than were enslaved in 1850, a decade before the Civil War began.

In the federal prison system alone, due in large part to new immigration laws, Latinos comprised 50.3 percent, Blacks 19.7 percent, and whites 26.4 percent of all people sentenced. And these numbers do not account for the millions more who are on parole or probation.

This is one of those gasoline-fueled infernos in desperate need of social reform rooted in social justice. Where is the compassion when we tolerate a system we know has been constructed to house generations of poor people of color?

We also know that generational poverty plays a role in the disproportionate number of Blacks and Hispanics now in jail. It's no coincidence that, as author Barbara Ehrenreich emphasized, the number of Americans residing in prisons (2.3 million) matches exactly the number of the poor living in public housing. A decisive study, "Incarceration & Social Inequality" by criminologists Bruce Western and Becky Pettit, found that more than 200,000 kids in the United States have a mother behind bars, and more than 1.7 million have a father in prison. These numbers accentuate the prison-poverty gravitational pull.[78]

Once trapped in the prison system, it is virtually impossible to escape the poverty pool. In *The New Jim Crow,* Alexander details how those who are released from prison and lucky enough to land a minimum-wage job are automatically required to pay back accumulated child support incurred while in prison, the cost of imprisonment—including court costs and processing fees—and, in some states, the cost of representation. With these dues being 100 percent garnishable, it's little wonder that 70 percent of former prisoners are returned to prison within three years.[79]

For decades, most Americans have turned a blind eye to the injustices of the justice system. What has not been given much thought, regrettably, is the link between poverty and prisons. Prison becomes a real possibility when people can't pay traffic fines, miss child support payments and court dates, and start bouncing checks. As previously stated, more than 6 million people rely on food stamps as their only source of income.

When faced with the decision to buy food or sell some of their stamps for gas, utility bills, or medicine, many honest Americans opt for the latter. In a *Colorlines* magazine article, "Selling Food Stamps for Kids Shoes" (February 16, 2010), writer Seth F. Wessler described how selling food stamps—an illegal act—has become a growing "survival mechanism."

Now that more Americans, particularly the middle class, are in the realm of poverty, they are shocked to find themselves in a cruel and compassion-less society that delights in punishing the poor.

THE POOR NEED NOT APPLY

> *"Pain and sorrow and misery have a right*
> *to our assistance: compassion puts us in mind*
> *of the debt, and that we owe it to ourselves*
> *as well as to the distressed."*
> —Joseph Butler

Just as technology has made it easier for Americans to disconnect from one another, it has also proved the culprit responsible for the disconnection between employers and employees.

"American business is about maximizing shareholder value," said Allen Sinai, chief global economist at the research firm Decision Economics. "You basically don't want workers. You hire less, and you try to find capital equipment to replace them."[80]

With profits as their only motivator, companies have increasingly cut workforces by exporting blue- and white-collar jobs to low-cost countries overseas. According to industry experts, some 5.6 million automation and manufacturing jobs have been outsourced since 2000.

Corporate fat cats don't see people; they see numbers—as in huge salaries and bonuses for saving money, cutting overhead, and making profits. With technology, they don't even have to look you in the eye to destroy your dreams. Most large companies now employ robovoices that direct applicants to the Internet to fill out an application. Desperate, you comply, hoping your keyboard can somehow convey your passion, charm, and expertise.

The corporate climate has become so cold that many large, callous companies now tell the unemployed that they need not even apply online if they've been out of work too long. According to Catherine Rampell of the New York Times, jobs calling . . . etc." for the "already employed" or "recently laid off" included hotel concierges, restaurant managers, teachers, I. T. specialists, analysts, account executives, salesmen, auditors, and many more.

Some states such as New Jersey and Illinois have challenged automated rejections based on long-term unemployment under the *Employment Advertisement Fairness Act*—which states that employers may not "publish in print or on the Internet an advertisement for a job that contains a statement indicating that current employment is a job qualification."

"This practice is simply wrong," wrote *Chicago Tribune's* Rex Huppke in his (September 2010) "I Just

Work Here" column. "At a time when millions of
Americans are frustrated and desperate and demoralized,
throwing up another roadblock to gainful employment
is reprehensible."

We couldn't have expressed it better. Gone are the
days of "boot-strap" lore when we were encouraged to
get tough, get out in the workforce, and aggressively
grab our slice of the American pie. Profits have overruled
the slogans, the boots are made in Asia, and the straps
can be found only online.

WHEN CHARITY AND PHILANTHROPY AREN'T ENOUGH

> *"Compassion brings us to a stop, and for a moment*
> *we rise above ourselves."*
> —Mason Cooley

Too often when we talk about compassion toward
the poor, we find ourselves using the language of charitable contribution and philanthropic giving. These are
beautiful and laudable efforts. But multinational companies that ship American jobs overseas make charitable donations. Billionaires and millionaires who pay
a smaller percentage of taxes than low-income workers
through tax breaks and loopholes can be philanthropic
with little compassion.

David and Charles Koch are good examples. The
brothers are worth about $21 billion each. With fortunes
gained mostly from the oil business, they are charitable
givers whose funding of the arts is indeed legendary.

We applaud, and benefit from, their generosity. But the Koch Brothers are also heavy funders of mean-spirited, right-wing individuals and groups hell-bent on eliminating social services that serve the poor.

Oftentimes when benevolent, rich, fellow citizens give to worthy charities, they are simultaneously supporting unjust institutions that profit from social misery. Charitable giving is not social justice.

By contrast, billionaire investor Warren Buffett seems to be a philanthropist intent on challenging the political structure that caters to those in his income bracket. In his August 14, 2011, *The New York Times* commentary, "Stop Coddling the Super-Rich," Buffett broke down some of the perks he and other members of the über-rich club enjoy. His income group pays only 17.4 percent on taxable income while the average worker pays 36 percent. In his commentary, Buffett described how the taxable income for the top 400 wage earners rose from $16.9 billion in 1992 to $90.9 billion in 2008. Yet, Buffett wrote, the rich actually paid a lower percentage (from 29.2 percent in 1992 to 21.5 percent in 2008) on their taxable income:

> "These and other blessings are showered upon us by legislators in Washington who feel compelled to protect us, much as if we were spotted owls or some other endangered species. It's nice to have friends in high places."

Microsoft mogul Bill Gates and other members of the "Giving Pledge"—where billionaires like Buffett have committed to give most of their wealth to philanthropy—should be applauded. Buffett, however, is one of the few who demonstrates compassion by challenging government to restructure tax laws that benefit folk like him, the richest of the rich.

A RENAISSANCE OF COMPASSION

How can we fulfill Walter Rauschenbusch's call for "justice for all, service to others, and a love that liberates" in the troubling 21st century? In these times of increasing scarcity when we can find little hope, there is a desperate need to resurrect social justice. We need leaders in the prophetic Christian tradition, like Rauschenbusch, King, and Gandhi. They must stoke the embers of righteous indignation into an almighty, inextinguishable blaze.

When it comes to poverty, America has adhered to "TINA" ("there is no alternative"), the slogan attributed to former British Prime Minister Margaret Thatcher. We propose replacing TINA with TIALA: "There is another loving alternative."

Here now we wish to ask the central question raised by the Reverend Dr. Mark Taylor: "Whatever happened to the notion of love in our public discourse?" We should perhaps define what we mean when we use the slippery term "love."

Love for us means everyone is worthy of a life of dignity and decency—just because. Not because of where they were born, who they know, where they live, where they were educated, where they work, or what the size of their annual income is. The sheer humanity of each and every one of us warrants our steadfast commitment to the well-being of each other.

This is what Dr. King had in mind when he suggested that justice is what love looks like in public.

This is what John Coltrane had in mind when he composed "A Love Supreme."

This is what Toni Morrison had in mind when she wrote *Beloved*.

This is what Dorothy Day had in mind when she embodied a dark and dangerous love.

This is what Nelson Mandela had in mind when he opted for justice over revenge.

This is what Rabbi Abraham Joshua Heschel had in mind when he spoke of the compassion of the Hebrew prophets.

This is what Mahmoud Mohamed Taha had in mind when he preached of the mercy of Allah.

This is what Mahatma Gandhi had in mind when he lived the loving soul force he talked about.

This is what that first-century Palestinian Jew named Jesus had in mind when he commanded us to love our neighbor as ourselves.

Lest we mislead you, this is not only about a loving

heart; rather, it is also about finding loving social (structural and institutional) alternatives to the nightmare of poverty that can be the dawning of a new day for poor people everywhere.

This new day must begin with a fresh imagination, a decision to discover some hard answers to some hard questions. Namely, what kind of person do we really want to be? Cowardly and complacent or courageous and compassionate? What kind of country do we really want to be? Cold-hearted and callous or caring and considerate?

The choice is ours.

CHAPTER 6

Poverty of Imagination

"But today our very survival depends on our ability to stay awake, to adjust to new ideas, to remain vigilant and to face the challenge of change.
The large house in which we live demands that we transform this worldwide neighborhood into a worldwide brotherhood [sisterhood]."

—Dr. Martin Luther King, Jr.,
Where Do We Go From Here?

"Those jobs aren't coming back."

Steve Jobs's frank reply probably wasn't something President Barack Obama wanted to hear. Apple, the company formerly headed by the late Steve Jobs, manufactures millions of iMacs, iPhones, iPads, and other products that are sold around the world but manufactured overseas.

During an exclusive dinner in California with Silicon Valley VIPs, including Jobs, the President asked how Apple manufacturing jobs could be brought back to America. Jobs's answer, according to several news sources, was no-nonsense. He told President Obama that the days of large-scale manufacturing in America were over because of inefficiency.[81]

As far as many profit-driven corporations and their subsidiaries are concerned, it's simply easier and cheaper to manufacture products in places like Asia and Latin America. The proof is in the products. Cell phones, Dell computers, televisions, vending machines, Nike and Converse tennis shoes, Mattel toys, Rawlings baseballs, Samsonite luggage, and Levi's jeans, are all manufactured overseas.[82]

What made America a superpower in the 19th century—industrialization and manufacturing—are now the economic engines that keep countries outside our borders pole-vaulting toward greatness.

Obama's question to Jobs and Jobs's response underscores an unprecedented 21st-century reality: Under the rules of contemporary capitalism, profit trumps people. It's highly unlikely that these manufacturing jobs will ever come back home. Corporate executives argue that they have to be lean and mean to survive in the global economy.

As economist Jeffrey Sachs commented on *Tavis Smiley:*

> "This is really the story of America, how the market system, especially in the global era, took away a lot of jobs in America that used to provide a middle class income, especially in the manufacturing sector. Instead of the government helping to create new skills, new industries, and so on, the government teamed with the most powerful and

richest interests in this country. That's how campaigns are made, and since those 30 years [they]
have continued to side with the top 1 percent and
totally ignore the bottom—the poorest people—
and once in a while say something about the
middle, but really only pay attention to the top."

Any CEO can say "jobs aren't coming back." But it
takes imagination and vision to determine *how* new jobs
can be created through American ingenuity in the information age. It seems the more techno-savvy, digitized,
and modernized our society becomes, the more the average American's imagination has declined. Increasingly,
we are victims of imaginative impotence. Poverty of vision has led to record unemployment, corporate avarice,
empty houses but homeless families, and dwindling
opportunities in a politically paralyzed nation. A lack of
bold, innovative ideas ensures that the rich will continue getting richer while the poor, the new poor, and the
former middle class will be handed a permanent sen-
tence to be served amid America's growing underclass.

REMAKING AMERICA

> *"There is a boundary to men's passions when they act
> from feelings; but none when they are under the influ-
> ence of imagination."*
> — Edmund Burke

Imagination unleashed can help transform America.
Uninhibited innovation can lay the foundation for
an equitable economy. With a surplus of vision we

can discover how to create jobs, rebuild communities, strengthen families, and offer productive alternatives that will reduce the ranks of the permanent poor and make poverty a revolving door that you pass through on your way to economic stability instead of a financial dead-end.

Reigniting our imaginations on this critical topic was the reason for convening the "Remaking America: From Poverty to Prosperity" symposium in January 2012. After our "Poverty Tour" ended, we were called to take what we saw, what we heard, and what impacted us deeply to the next level. We set out to establish a new level of awareness about contemporary poverty that could catalyze the kinds of discussions necessary to create changes in policy and in our society. With an expressed intent to get this issue higher up on the American agenda, we invited some of the most pre-eminent voices of our time to join us in a discussion about the factors that led to the Great Recession and the ever-widening gap between the rich and the poor. Most importantly, we wanted to spark the kind of conversation that has to catch fire from the lowest to the highest rungs of our society if we are to make the journey from "poverty to prosperity" a 21st-century reality.

Panelist Barbara Ehrenreich explained the corporate mind-set that has the economy stuck in neutral:

> "All the rewards in our form of capitalism have been for the people at the top who can reduce the number of employees they have. That's all they know how to do."

Capitalism, she added, may be self-imploding:

"It's destroying itself. This can't work. You can't have an economic system where fewer and fewer people can participate as either workers or consumers because they don't earn enough or they don't have jobs. You can't run things like this. It's not a matter of do we like capitalism or not; it's a matter of how do we survive when that isn't working anymore."

Acclaimed finance expert Suze Orman, another symposium panelist, echoed Ehrenreich's sentiments:

"What keeps us in poverty is . . . there's a highway into poverty and there's no longer even a sidewalk out. To get out of poverty you have to have a source of income. You have to have the ability to generate money so that you are not poor. It is not brain science. You cannot make money if there isn't a job for you . . . even if you do make money, you can't afford to pay for things, especially when you see the prices of food out there and what it costs."

Another thing that keeps us in poverty is the word itself, "poverty": how we define it, how we think about it, how we run from it, and how we've failed to address it adequately in the past. We can't defeat a 21st-century problem with a 19th- or 20th-century arsenal. The Great Recession has provided another one of those once-in-a-lifetime moments for evolutionary change. Sadly, it has taken the new face of poverty—the downward-spiraling middle class—to move Americans to talk about poverty in a substantive way. With righteous indignation, people-powered motivation, and reignited imagination, we can create an equitable and just American economy and finally end the denial that has allowed poverty to grow so exponentially.

LEADER OR LEADERLESS?

"It is logical that the United States should do whatever it is able to do to assist in the return of normal economic health in the world, without which there can be no political stability and no assured peace."
—George Marshall, U.S. Secretary of State

In 1947, two years after the end of World War II, Europe was in shambles and economic disaster reigned. Industrial production was low and unemployment was astronomically high. Famine was rampant and millions were unemployed, starving, homeless, and living in abject poverty.

President Harry S. Truman signed the European Recovery Program (ERP), better known as "The Marshall Plan," named after Truman's Secretary of State, George Marshall. In making the case for European aid before Congress on March 12, 1947, Truman used compassionate language and a pragmatic appeal:

"The seeds of totalitarian regimes are nurtured by misery and want. They spread and grow in the evil soil of poverty and strife. They reach their full potential when the hope of a people for a better life has died. We must

keep that hope alive. If we falter in our leadership, we may endanger the peace of the world—and we shall surely endanger the welfare of our own nation."

With those words and more, President Truman made Europe's tragedy the world's tragedy. He engaged minds, hearts, and imaginations and challenged Congress to see themselves as protectors of the nation's welfare. Three months later, Marshall struck a similar chord during a commencement speech delivered on June 5, 1947, at Harvard University:

"Our policy is directed not against any country or doctrine but against hunger, poverty, desperation, and chaos. Its purpose should be the revival of a working economy in the world so as to permit the emergence of political and social conditions in which free institutions can exist."

Note the key phrases: *"hunger, poverty, desperation, and chaos"* and *"revival of a working economy."* The ERP— at a cost of $12.5 billion—helped increase Western Europe's industrial production by 30 percent within four years. Although America had international partners, the ERP was the result of bold political imagination and leadership. America was that audacious world leader who saw Europe's conditions of unemployment and famine as a genuine threat to democracy.[83]

Here we are, almost 65 years after the Marshall Plan, and an increasing portion of our citizens are besieged with unemployment, poverty, and hunger. Where is the American Marshall Plan? Where are today's political leaders in the tradition of Truman and Marshall?

What are our priorities? Where are the fearless men and women who are strong enough and courageous enough to take a stand against income inequality?

There was an interesting interplay on this topic between symposium panelists Barbara Ehrenreich and Suze Orman. Ehrenreich said:

> "I want to see the discussion move past leaders, whether we're talking about the ones in Congress and in the White House, so-called leaders, or whoever. We took a huge leap in the last few months when we had a proud and leaderless movement. What did that mean? Was that crazy? Was that nuts? No. That meant everybody becomes a leader. I'm going to say we've discovered something in the last few months which is much bigger than the power of any individual, leader, or otherwise, and that is the power of solidarity. People working together . . . that is our greatest strength."

Orman maintained that it is the power of one that must first be harnessed to build the kind of unified power and solidarity that Ehrenreich seeks:

> "To come out of poverty, you also need hope. You need to believe that you can come out of poverty. If one person can make a move towards it and help lift everybody else out, then you start to get the solidarity. But if you all keep thinking there's nothing I can do, it doesn't matter, then there's no hope."

Both women summoned the truth. It took a visionary with no vision, Helen Keller, to challenge the cruel and inhumane treatment of the blind and handicapped. Struck deaf and blind at the age of 19 months, Keller became one of the world's most influential and passionate voices for the physically impaired and disenfranchised. She was a suffragist, pacifist, socialist, co-founder of the American Civil Liberties Union (ACLU), and an early supporter of birth control. She joined with like-minded others to advance the causes she valued the most. Keller traveled internationally and testified before Congress to raise awareness and advocate for the blind and handicapped.

It took the victory of one oppressed man to inspire the multitude and dismantle the oppressive apartheid system in South Africa. After 27 years in prison on charges of treason, Nelson Mandela emerged, resolve unbroken, as a symbol of resistance that inspired Black South Africans and the world. In 1990, South African president F. W. de Klerk ordered the release of Mandela. Still fiercely active at the age of 72, Mandela led negotiations with the minority government that resulted in the end of apartheid and the beginning of a multiracial government. In 1994, Mandela was elected South Africa's president in the country's first free election.

Keller's and Mandela's stories prove that, yes, one unbound imagination, one individual, can become the inspiration for millions, as Orman said. But Ehrenreich's point, that the movement to end poverty will more than likely be a "leaderless" movement, is a powerful reflection of the times that we live in. Revolution in the information age demands a new model. There are no exemptions in the body politic; everybody has been hit by various forms of financial distress—from retirees fleeced by Bernie Madoff, to auto workers in Detroit, retirees in Florida, and municipal workers in Wisconsin. Poverty in the 21st century has taught us many lessons— but first and foremost, we have discovered that poverty is an equal opportunity employer and that we are all vulnerable to unpredictable economic maelstroms. Like all powerful social movements, this effort won't be led by a single person, but it will be advanced by a single message.

BLESS THE MAJORITY

> *"I don't want to remember 2005 as a year that*
> *the government heaped unnecessary burdens*
> *upon American families. Stealing from the poor*
> *and middle class and giving to the rich,*
> *while increasing the deficit, is hardly responsible."*
>
> —Samuel Dash

Although political leadership is crucial, we aren't naïve enough to believe that politicians, dependent on the rich to even get to Washington, will lead this revolution. In an interview on *Tavis Smiley* on PBS, Jeffrey Sachs recalled his reaction in 2008 when he learned the Obama administration was going to compromise its pledge to end the Bush-era tax cuts for wealthy Americans:

"I was shocked. I sent a note to them: 'What are you doing?'

"I know as an economist if we don't tax the rich so that we can rebuild schools, so that we can rebuild neighborhoods, so that we can focus on real infrastructure projects, not shovel-ready, which don't exist, but real infrastructure over a decade, we're not going to be able to rebuild, we're not going to have the skills, we're not going to create good jobs."[84]

Although the majority of Americans, according to survey polls at the time, were in favor of letting the tax codes expire, Sachs explained how politics in 2010 took precedence:

"All of a sudden there's a deal between the White House and the Congress to extend them for two more years. That wasn't because the President's back was to the wall; sadly not, because 60 percent of Americans wanted the top tax rates to go up. They know what the story is. But that's not what the political advisers were saying. 'No, no, you can't do that, you're running for reelection. You're going to need the campaign contributions.'"

As Alex Gourevitch and Aziz Rana argued in their February 2012 Salon.com article "America's Failed Promise of Equal Opportunity," both Democrats and Republicans are tethered to a class-based, "early 21st-century version of social mobility." It is a version that defines equal opportunity as the ability "to rise into the few positions of social power and prestige, or perhaps more broadly, into the economically secure, high earning professions."

America has always been made stronger when fed-up, diverse, powerless people were forced to fight for democracy. Once again, we have arrived at that time-honored crossroad. And, as symposium panelist Michael Moore passionately articulated, most Americans are on board:

> "This is a country where the majority wants the rich to pay their fair share of taxes. The majority wants the regulations put back on Wall Street. The majority wants somebody arrested for the crash of '08 and put in jail. That's what the majority wants. Bless the majority."

WATCH YOUR MOUTH

Have you ever given thought to those curbside cut-ins on America's streets? Bikers use them, baby strollers and luggage-pushers use them. We use them at hotels, restaurants, airports, and more. Well, they weren't made for everyone. They were designed for the handicapped, but we all benefit. The same applies to the civil rights struggle—Black people benefited but so too did women, Latinos, Asians, and other minority groups.

We bring up the curbside cut-ins and the Civil Rights Movement to make two points related to the current battle. First, when poverty ends, everybody wins— the economy of the nation as a whole, all classes, races, creeds, and neighborhoods. Second, to achieve this goal, it's necessary to change outmoded 20th-century mind-sets, perceptions, and attitudes as we dare to bring the subject of poverty into the mainstream.

At one time, the disabled, like the poor, suffered

massive discrimination. They were separated from families, locked away in institutions and asylums, barred from public schools, and barely tolerated in polite society. Negative labels, such as "imbecile," "cripple," "deaf and dumb," were applied without dispute—and the result was that the mentally and physically challenged were judged as "damaged goods" and rejected throughout society.

Yet, through advocacy, leadership, and persistence, great strides were made that led to the enactment of the *Americans with Disabilities Act* (ADA) in 1990, which prohibited discrimination based on disabilities. When signing the bill into law, President George Herbert Walker Bush declared that "the shameful wall of exclusion must finally come tumbling down" and make way for "a bright new era of equality, independence, and freedom." Before the ADA became law, attitudes had to change and the lexicon had to shift. Referring to someone as a "cripple" was no longer acceptable. "Handicapped" became the new vernacular for the disabled.

Another example of affirming the humanity of a marginalized group was achieved when the language and attitudes were challenged and changed with regard to the lesbian, gay, bisexual, and transgender (LGBT) peoples.

The successes of the handicapped and the LGBT community speak to the hard work required for societal transformation. Before we can get people to seriously consider the end of poverty, we have to shred destructive misconceptions. Ending poverty is not only about saving the impoverished in the ghetto, barrio, or reservation.

It's also about helping the citizens who find themselves living in America's "great middle" and are now struggling for resources to find their way.

We need to reframe the dialogue. But before we dream of an America without poverty, we must dare to change our minds.

THE BIG MISTAKE

"If the misery of the poor be caused not by the laws of nature, but by our institutions, great is our sin."
—Charles Darwin

People of color have historically been the targets of practices such as housing redlining, subprime lending, high interest loans, and other exploitative, opportunistic, big-business manipulations. Symposium panelist Roger Clay, President of the Insight Center for Community Economic Development in Oakland, California, spoke to this:

"Black folks have been hurting for a long, long, long time. But no one paid attention to it because we look at the unemployment rate for everybody and not for various sub-populations. What's happening now is that there are a lot of white folks that have fallen out of the middle class who are in danger."

We dare to imagine a world where our red, brown, Black, and yellow brothers and sisters have the same value as our white brothers and sisters, but we also welcome truth—no matter what road brought us here. And, according to Michael Moore, most Americans are of one mind because the rich, the corporate puppeteers, and the greedy made a huge miscalculation:

> "The mistake they've made, just to deal with the racial part of this, is their boot has been on the necks of people of color since we began. They had a permanent poor class, mostly of people of color, but a lot of poor white people, too. They had a permanent class of poor that they could use as essentially a threat to the middle class. If you asked for too much, if you asked for higher wages, if you expected health benefits . . . you could very quickly be over there with 'those people.' They knew how to manipulate this group."

As the polls and surveys we mentioned earlier indicate, prior to the recession, most of the middle class were ambivalent about the rich/poor divide and thoroughly convinced they, too, could be rich. Conservative politicians played on these unreal expectations and got voters to support trickle-down theories and to resist tax hikes on the rich. But, as Moore asserted, Wall Street bankers and lenders overplayed their hand:

> "The huge catastrophic tactical mistake they made—because of their incredible greed—was, after they soaked the poor . . . they thought: 'Geez, we're just not making enough money. What can we get off the middle class? Wait a minute, they all own homes. Let's do the mortgage thing.'"

The middle class has always enjoyed the luxury of buying and living in decent homes, summer vacations, and sending their children to college. Now, Moore continued, "The system says 'we're taking that away from you.' Well, now there's hell to pay."

"They went after them, they went after their homes. They moved their jobs overseas. They took their healthcare away. They made it so that their children would be the first generation in the history of this country who would be worse off than their parents' generation."

America's elite, like dictators and plutocrats in the Arab world, also fell victim to outdated 20th-century thinking. For decades, the rich and the powerful controlled how their countries and regimes were projected around the world. These regimes were unprepared for uprisings fueled by advancing technologies' upstart and uncontrollable offspring—social media. It was Facebook postings, Twitter tweets, and other technological tools that engaged the world and legitimized the revolts in Tunisia, Yemen, Egypt, and elsewhere.

In America, the wealthy one percent now find themselves in the grip of a highly contagious social-media campaign ignited by five undeniable and powerful words:

"We are the 99 percent!"

BREAKING FREE

"Imagination will often carry us to worlds that never were. But without it, we go nowhere."
—Carl Sagan

Throughout American history, there have been proud moments of revolution that forced the elite to remove their blinders of greed, tyranny, and domination. A powerful British monarchy was blind to the unfair taxation and denial of basic liberties that bred revolt in the colonies. It took a bloody American revolution to seed liberty, freedom, and democracy in the New World's soil. Unprecedented wealth, fueled by the unpaid labor of slaves, blinded the Founding Fathers and the oppressive white majority to the inhumanity written into the U.S. Constitution. It took a righteous abolitionist revolt against American slavery to right that insidious wrong.

America has since made great strides for freedom in regard to all of its citizens. But now America has regressed: Poverty is the new slavery, and oligarchs are the new kings. The blinders are once again firmly affixed, and the necessary checks and balances have disappeared. Taxation without representation is now reflected in policies that allow the wealthy to be coddled and under-taxed while the perennially poor, working poor, and "new poor" are ignored and rendered invisible.

It is time to reawaken American democracy. It is time for a nonviolent, democratic revolution. It is time for righteous indignation against the fleecing of America's poor. And there is no time like the present, given the indifference toward the poor that has infected our political discourse.

In early 2012, Republican presidential hopeful Mitt Romney uttered the blunderous words: "I'm not concerned about the very poor," voicing the sentiments of too many Americans. Still Romney underestimated the reactions of Americans who now find themselves "very poor." Many of these individuals were looking for direction from the candidate, not disdain.

Right-wing loyalists and pundits have tried in vain to cloud the discussion of economic parity by identifying it as "class envy." They defensively suggest that somehow people are simply hatin' on folk who have all the money and favors afforded to them by politicians, lobbyists, and sweetheart tax codes.

"It's not envy, it's a class war. It's a war that has been perpetrated by the rich onto everybody else," filmmaker Moore stated. "Class war is the one they started."

Symposium panelist Jeffrey Sachs added that the "war on the poor" escalated when the government bailed out Wall Street.

"What's amazing is that in 2008, when Wall Street created a worldwide disaster, these CEOs, these titans of finance that nearly wrecked the world, said, 'What? Me? No, we want government bailouts, give us a trillion.' Then with that money they paid themselves more billions of bonuses the next year." Sachs continued, sharing parts of his conversation with Larry Summers, then head of the National Economic Council: "What are you doing? You're letting them take taxpayer money for their mega-bonuses."

Summers, the economic adviser from Wall Street, countered, "Well, Jeff, where would you draw the line?" Sachs answered, "Larry . . . it's taxpayer money going out in big bonuses. But Wall Street and politics are so tightly infused they couldn't even draw the line at that moment, and that's why we've reached a point where Wall Street abused the public, it abused the trust, it violated the laws, because every one of our big firms, whether it's Goldman Sachs or Merrill Lynch or JP Morgan, they're paying fines right now for what they did against the securities laws, and yet they've remained in charge."

The Occupy Wall Street key slogan, "We are the 99 percent," is "rigorously accurate," Sachs said. While "the rich have never been richer," the government continues to give them preference while gutting services that poor people need for education, health care, and other vital necessities. Because the top 1 percent walked away with the prize, struggling Americans are fed up. This is why, he reasoned, people are out in the streets protesting across the country:

> "The 400 richest people in this country, the billionaires on the new *Forbes* list, have more than $1 trillion of wealth. They're averaging more than $3.5 billion, each of them, in their net worth, and then we're told by Washington politicians, 'Oh, there's nothing we can do; we have a budget crisis.' Well, sure. If you let the richest of the richest of the rich just walk scot-free, bear no responsibility in our society, then there won't be [anything] for the poorest of the poor.

> "People whom we have seen, you, Tavis, have seen on the tour, and whose voice you're bringing to America, they're suddenly realizing, 'Wait a minute—this isn't a market economy, just good luck and bad luck. These guys broke the rules, they

broke the law. They took the money, they sided with politics, and they're still there. What kind of market system is that?' That's a rigged system, and that's what people are starting to wake up to."

It's not only a "rigged" and outdated system, it's tragically broken. This "war" isn't personal or political, it's about systemic transformation. It's a war in need of soldiers of every color, of every creed, and every political persuasion—anyone who's concerned enough to take a risk, pay a cost, live, and maybe die so that our children won't be destroyed by a poisonous system. This is why the movement must focus on bodies, minds, hearts, and souls who have the imagination and courage to come together, organize, and reactivate the legacies of leaders who have dared to face poverty down.

SEEING AHEAD

*"You can't depend on your eyes
when your imagination is out of focus."*
—Mark Twain

"What recession?"
This was the response we heard when we visited our indigenous brothers and sisters in Lac Courte Oreilles Indian Reservation in Hayward, Wisconsin. Poverty, unemployment, and early death from diseases such as cancer and diabetes have been a mainstay on the reservation for decades. Rick St. Germaine, a history professor who grew up in a log cabin during the late 1940s at Lac Courte Oreilles said it wasn't until 1960 that electricity

and paved roads found their way to the reservation.

We turn to the Native Americans of Lac Courte Oreilles to underscore a painful truth. Disproportionate poverty, unemployment, and the exploitation of people of color have been ignored in America for centuries. Nevertheless, the resilient poor have found ways to withstand the long storm of collective poverty.

During our visit at Lac Courte Oreilles, Councilmember Russell "Rusty" Barber told us how the residents on the 80,000-acre reservation have survived and created a sustainable community: by pooling resources and using revenues generated by casinos to create low-wage jobs that include health-care benefits, that fund schools, and that address the needs of elder tribesmen.

We're certainly not advocating for more gambling casinos, but as we wrote in Chapter Four, "Poverty of Courage," if oppression doesn't kill you, it will demand innovation. As in desperate times of yesteryear, the dispossessed are coming up with imaginative ways— some legal, others not so much—to address the crisis of poverty while still attempting to hold the government accountable for the safety and well-being of its citizenry. Their voices, methods of survival and imaginations are crucial in shaping their—and our—destiny.

REMAKING AMERICA

*"You never change things by fighting the existing reality.
To change something, build a new model
that makes the existing model obsolete."*
—R. Buckminster Fuller

Since business leaders have prioritized the path to profit at all costs and opted to transport American jobs overseas, we have no choice but to explore other ways to create jobs in our own communities and insist that the government create immediate job opportunities for all categories of the "poor."

MacArthur Genius Grant winner and host of the public radio program *The Promised Land,* Majora Carter, shared her unique perspective during our symposium:

"We're not going to abolish capitalism tomorrow. But we can come up with ways to create new opportunities in our inner cities, in our rural areas, in poor areas that really desperately need the kind of places, the kind of economic development that's going to support poor people and help move them out of poverty and actually allow them to experience the American Dream."

If middle class jobs aren't coming back, Carter envisions construction jobs that improve Americans' quality of life:

"The fact that we can use environmentally sound ways to support things like storm water management and energy conservation while creating real jobs that provide us opportunities, accessible jobs in particular for people who have been left behind by our education system for so long. Whether it's green roofing and urban forestry management . . . these type of things actually help improve air quality. They help create lower energy bills as well. A cooler city means you use less energy, especially in the summertime."

Carter's vision, though environmentally and economically sound, still requires imagination that's sorely lacking among private investors and public officials. It's hard to imagine a divided Congress that's bent on the destruction of political enemies ever coming to consensus on a federally backed Green jobs initiative for the nation's urban or rural areas.

This is one of the reasons that New York City Public Advocate Bill de Blasio has proposed a radical idea that's not dependent on federal resources. Instead, it is based on the use of the city's pension funds to stimulate the local economy.

"We know the federal government is not going to be there for us in the way we would like in New York City. We have a very troubled infrastructure, and fixing this economic infrastructure will decide New York's future," De Blasio told NPR radio host Brian Lehrer of *The Brian Lehrer Show* on WNYC in February 2012. According to de Blasio, there's no way that either political party will end up with a majority in Congress—even after the 2012 elections—that will bring about the balance necessary to break the logjam in Washington. Meanwhile, the Economic Policy Institute reports that the city of New York has an 8.8 percent unemployment rate, while Black New Yorkers have an unemployment rate of 13.3 percent and Hispanics 8.7 percent. The city's union has $100 billion in pension investments that it can tap into for public project investments. The union has the authorization to

use about $1.2 billion of those funds for housing proj-
ects. Under his proposal, about $400 million would go
toward affordable housing developments and another
$800 million would be targeted to infrastructure projects
on bridges, roads, schools, and the like.

"This is the shape of things to come," De Blasio
told Lehrer. "Use publicly controlled assets to maximize
economic activity and do some of the things that are
not going to happen due to the failure on other levels of
government."

Ironically, the poor have already moved in the do-
for-self-without-government-help direction. They've
occupied public land and foreclosed homes. They've
shared space, utilities, and food costs. In a way, they've
tapped into the contemporary eco-village model where
individuals with shared social, economic, and ecologi-
cal concerns and resources have built interdependent,
efficient, low-maintenance communities.

Perhaps this model of shared community living
may prove to be both necessary and beneficial in today's economy. Twenty-first-century families with their
variety of configurations might benefit from pooling
their resources and buying a recently foreclosed multi-
unit property at a reasonable price. They could share the
mortgage note, transportation, utilities, and child-care
responsibilities. Or tend a backyard garden, grow nutri-
tious food, save grocery money, and provide healthy
meals for the families.

With imagination, we can stem the decline of stable
and long-neglected neighborhoods. Perhaps bankers
who caused the housing crisis should focus less energy

on foreclosures and more on helping homeowners and low-skill or no-skill workers to rebuild abandoned communities.

During our televised symposium, Roger Clay talked about a two-tier approach to economic restoration: "The immediate is jobs in the public sector, jobs in the private sector, supporting businesses, especially small businesses and micro-businesses. Then we have to start working on our systems that create poverty and keep people in poverty, like our educational system and our criminal justice system."

HUNGRY IN AMERICA

It was no surprise that hunger in America and food scarcity were on the mind of Vicki B. Escarra, President and CEO of Feeding America, the nation's leading domestic hunger-relief charity, during our *Remaking America* symposium:

> "While we're working on the longer term and as we think about poverty and all the things that really affect and are a part of poverty, hunger is the one issue that is solvable in our country."

It's "criminal," Escarra told us, when 17 million kids in this country go to school hungry every day. Malnutrition affects how they comprehend, behave, learn, and excel at school. Surely, this is a solvable problem, Escarra insisted:

> "There's enough food produced in America not only to feed every person in this country but also

most of the developed world. What I would do is find a way to work on the food system so that we can get what farmers grow to the plates of people that need food."

Working on the food system could be another cost-effective way to generate jobs, Escarra explained: "Actually it's giving dollars back as people try to get on their feet. If you don't have to worry about groceries, then you can get back on your feet." Designing a new food-creation and supply system calls for political accord and government involvement and resources.

Some experts predict that the economy will bounce back and be strong enough to repair the damage inflicted by the Great Recession. Robert Kagan, a senior fellow at the Brookings Institution and *Washington Post* columnist, has urged worried Americans to turn to history to calm their fears:

> "The United States has gone through these crises almost once every 40 years. We had a Great Depression in the 1890s, we had a Great Depression in the 1930s; we had the economic energy crisis in the 1970s; and here we are 40 years later," Kagan explained in a May 15, 2008, interview on *Charlie Rose* on PBS. "What's interesting is if you go back and look at those periods, the next decade of each of those economic periods, the United States came roaring back and was actually stronger relative to the rest of the world before."

Much of the commentary on America's decline, Kagan and other economists claim, doesn't take America's military clout and influence or other economic factors around the world into consideration. Even in these rough times, Kagan said, the United States still produces roughly one-quarter of the world's economic output and remains the largest and "richest economy in the world." Many economic advisers claim that the pendulum may be swinging back in America's direction. Their predictions are based largely on the rising cost of labor in China and the exorbitant costs of shipping products back to the United States. Also, ironically, it's becoming cheaper to manufacture goods in the United States, thanks to the recalibration of labor union benefits that have allowed companies to shrink wages and benefits in exchange for full employment for American workers.

We're not economists, but we believe that such lofty predictions are based on 20th-century thinking. First, our history of bouncing back is no indication that we will come back more vibrant after this unprecedented Great Recession. Second, relying on our military muscle to change the economic equation will fatten the purses only of the military industrial complex, waste more resources and lives, and wind up costing the American taxpayer more. Last, it's a sad commentary when our economy's resurrection is based on lower wages and fewer benefits for workers already stripped of the basic necessities as they attempt to dig themselves out of debt and raise their families.

Despite the daily predictions of economic recovery, our modern reality takes us to that challenging "what if" place. "What if" we can't count on the wealthy corporations or even the government to dig us out of this economic morass? What will become of our communities, our homes, and our children's future? Unlike previous generations, our 21st-century challenges demand a new collective vision and a return to larger measures of self-sufficiency.

DO-FOR-SELF . . . WITH A LITTLE HELP

We do not debate that fact that American innovation has allowed ailing economies to bounce back and stagnant societies to grow quickly. Such vision has created jobs when old ones became obsolete. Gone are the days when famous scientists and inventors such as Samuel F. B. Morse (telegraph), Alexander Graham Bell (telephone), and Thomas Alva Edison (household electricity and many other inventions) empowered the world with imagination. Yet here we are, only two decades into a digital revolution that has impacted every aspect of American life.

In a very real sense, no matter which recovery prognosticators you believe, now's the time to hold the government accountable while simultaneously holding ourselves accountable as we regain the capacity to "do-for-self." At the January 2012 symposium, Suze Orman emphasized "personal responsibility" and learning "how to make more out of less" as necessary strategies for survival in the new economy.

"You need to know what to do with money, who to give it to, how to invest it in your retirement plans, and how to be able to take care of yourself in the future," Orman cautioned. "Because my biggest fear is that they're just going to keep pushing all of this down the road. You're not going to have Medicare. You're not going to have Social Security in the way that you think it's going to be. You're not going to have pensions from the companies that you are working with."

Consequently, many believe America is headed for tougher economic times. There is no such phenomenon as a "jobless recovery." But before we envision new communities, we must first save homes in crisis and help people move out of poverty.

"The housing market isn't going to come back until the job market comes back," says Orman. "However, I do not understand why all the people who hold the mortgages, why we just don't reduce every single mortgage out there on every single home in America to the fair market value of that home today so the people that have homes and want to stay in their homes—they can't help it that they're under water and to no fault of their own. Why can't they take a $700,000 home in Tampa . . . and make it a $100,000 mortgage because that's what it could be sold for today? I don't understand why they are not willing to do that."

We assume that Orman meant banks when she referred to "they." If so, the answer is obvious: Because of greed, banks will do only what they are forced to do. Banks represent another antiquated system in need of drastic overhaul.

The full spectrum of America's middle class is now confronting new barriers that make economic survival even more challenging. One of the most devastating damages done to those who thought they were playing by the rules is the destruction of Americans' credit scores during the economic downturn.

"Through no fault of your own, in my belief, you've lost your home, you've lost your car, you've lost your job, you've lost everything, you've lost your ability to pay, they've taken everything away from you, and they've even taken your FICO score away. Now you are really FICO'd!" Orman joked. "Without a score—or a good score—if you happen to own a car, no matter what kind of car, your car insurance premiums are high. Landlords will not rent to you. Employers are starting not to hire you. If you want to do anything to change [your] situation, good luck . . . if you happen to get a loan, it will be at the highest interest rates possible."

Panelist Roger Clay's agency, Insight Center for Community Economic Development, published *Laying the Foundation for National Prosperity: The Imperative of Closing the Racial Wealth Gap.* This report also addressed the FICO score issue. It called for the creation of a "transparent, accurate, and fair" federal public credit scoring system with "flexible measures" that fairly determine a consumer's creditworthiness. This new system, the report advises, should consider rental payments, review the credit history of immigrants from their countries of origin, and account for the lack of debt.

WHEN PASSION MEETS POLICY

PolicyLink, Half in Ten, the Center for American Progress (CAP), The Food Trust, and many other unsung nonprofit agencies and progressive think tanks have been examining the problems of income inequality in America for decades. They have talked to and ministered to the vulnerable, researched ideas, created revolutionary models, and outlined job initiatives ready for implementation.

What's missing, however, is the political will that can be fueled only by the power of the people to bust through partisan blockades to institute a United States Marshall Plan tailored to the information age. Relevant jobs and minimum living-wage increases could bring immediate relief to America's new and old poor. This brings us full circle to the one leader vs. a leaderless movement debate for societal transformation. Just as Dr. King pushed President Johnson, just as Eleanor Roosevelt pushed FDR to be able to see the poor, Frederick Douglass challenged President Lincoln to give freedom to the slaves.

Douglas possessed the imagination and the far-seeing eyes that fortified Lincoln's political will to dismantle the institution of slavery. Douglass wasn't the only one encouraging emancipation, but he was the only former slave who had Lincoln's ear and who personally encouraged Lincoln to imagine what many considered unimaginable.

There is a reason that the bold civil rights demonstrations and traditional Black leadership voices aren't having the same effect in the 21st century as they did in the past. America's first Black President and a fractured Black body politic have changed the rules of engagement. Out of deference to the President, the prophetic legacy of speaking truth to power and bearing witness to the suffering of poor people has been stifled and nearly silenced. The multi-class, multicultured impact of widespread poverty dictates a multidimensional response. It is a fire ignited by youth, but one that must be stoked by a matured collective unaccustomed to microwave-fast results. Youthful energy and passion mixed with seasoned collaboration is a combustible agent for explosive change.

We face great challenges, but traversing them is the only path to great social justice. Changing perceptions of the poor, challenging the stereotypes that cause many to recoil from the very thought of being "poor," and galvanizing the individual and collective will necessary to stimulate political will are all daunting tasks.

We can boldly imagine the unimaginable only if history serves as our touchstone.

CHAPTER 7

The Poverty Manifesto

There are nearly 150 million persistently poor and near poor people in America who are not responsible for the damage done by the Great Recession. Yet they pay the price. The poor did not create the deindustrialization of America, unmatched corporate profiteering and greed, more than a decade of foreign wars, and unregulated tax benefits for the wealthy. When the largest economic institutions in the world were brought to their collective knees, they went crawling to the government's doorstep in search of salvation. The government obliged, allowing Wall Street to socialize its failure on the backs of Main Street Americans. The housing and jobs crisis they created fostered a poverty unseen in generations—not just in inner-city ghettos and barrios, but also in suburbs crossing all racial, age, and gender lines.

Nearly one-third of the American middle class—mostly families with children—have fallen into poverty.

The aftershock of the current economic downturn in reality was a pre-recession tremor rumbling under the surface for at least the past three decades. While the incomes of the richest 1 percent of Americans—those making $380,000 or more—has grown 33 percent in the past 20 years, incomes for 90 percent of Americans—the rest of us—have stagnated or declined. According to IRS data, the average income in 2008 was $33,000. Twenty years prior, the average American in 1988 earned $33,400, adjusted for inflation.

Despite talk of the job market's seeming recovery, it remains harder than ever to find work in America. For many, having a job is still not enough. Even as corporate profits have soared (with 40 percent going to big banks), more adults are in poverty than ever before. Middle class jobs are vanishing. In 2011, high-wage industries accounted for only 14 percent of new jobs. Meanwhile, low-wage work made up almost half of all the job growth. Close to 9 million people said they were working part-time only because they could not find full-time employment.

We can no longer judge anyone who is living poor in America as someone who is lazy or who has made a series of avoidable bad choices. Such pat indictments and stereotypes obscure a fundamental truth: there is a poverty of opportunity in America. America no longer has enough work for able-bodied people, and too many working people are not paid a living wage. The catastrophic downward spiral created by the Great Recession and exacerbated by unfair tax exemptions on America's wealthiest 1 percent has now sentenced millions to the unenviable ranks of those who have lost the ability to earn a living in America.

Indulging our outmoded shame-and-blame poverty paradigms keeps us all peddling acceptable lies about poverty. These lies keep us safe and comfortable and willing to write off poverty as a character failure, or the result of addiction, mental illness, or a criminal past. We want to pin the tail on any available donkey that will keep us from having to define poverty as "being unable to make a living because we can't find a job."

LONG LIVE THE LIE

For at least the past four decades, most Americans have been able to ignore the poor and deny the extent of poverty. Middle class people would disparage low-income people, low-income people would dog the working poor, and the working poor would beat down on the homeless poor—because we all want to feel like we have some sort of stature in life.

Be it shame and blame or utter disdain, all these attitudes were justified by stereotypes, distortions, and lies about the poor. It took the Great Recession to make poverty a real threat to the American psyche. When folk who didn't fit the stereotype started losing their businesses, jobs, and homes, and had to rely on government handouts, they took notice.

Our fear is that this recognition of poverty is temporary. Headlines trumpeting a boost in manufacturing and exports, or an uptick in the stock market, or lower jobless rates will lull many Americans back to the land of comfortable stereotyping and demonizing the poor.

Superficial snapshot indicators merely postpone a confrontation with the inevitable. America is no longer the indisputable world leader in innovation, manufacturing, and production. Worse yet, premature post-recession celebrations mean that we've blown another opportunity to really grapple with and solve the over-arching problem of poverty.

Throughout this book, we've documented the history of poverty in America and the ambitious starts, abrupt stops, and agonizing downturns in its elimination. Lies have a life of their own. Once circulated, they spread and grow; they become enshrined facts. Just ask President Obama, who spent the majority of his term refuting the vicious lie that he wasn't born on American soil or that he is a Muslim. And we can definitively say he is not a socialist.

Our intent with *The Rich and the Rest of Us* is to make us think about the pervasiveness of poverty, its real causation, and the threat it poses to our democracy. We want to raise awareness about poverty and discuss how best to end it—in our lifetime. But before we can launch a strategic plan, we must first address the big lies about poverty.

TEN LIES ABOUT POVERTY THAT AMERICA CAN NO LONGER AFFORD

1. **Poverty is a character flaw.**
   False. Poverty is the lack of money—period. The 150 million Americans in or near poverty are there as a result of unemployment, war, the Great Recession, corporate greed, and income inequality.

2. **American manufacturing is going to bounce back.**
   False: The United States has lost an average of 50,000 manufacturing jobs every month since 2001. Today, China dominates the global manufacturing industry and has no intention of releasing its title as "the world's top manufacturer."

3. **The Great Recession has ended.**
   Not really: Most of the new jobs created since "economic recovery" began have been low-wage occupations. While 60 percent of the jobs lost during the economic downturn were in mid-wage occupations, 73 percent of the jobs added have been in lower-wage occupations such as cashiers, stock clerks, and food preparation workers. The Post Office, once a middle class safe haven for nonskilled workers, recently announced a downsizing plan that will eliminate 35,000 jobs. Where and how will those workers be absorbed in the new economy?

4. **Minorities receive the majority of government entitlements.**
   False: Nearly half (48.5 percent) of all Americans,

live in a household that received some type of government benefit in the first quarter of 2010, according to Census data. Seventy percent of food stamp recipients are white.

5. **No one goes hungry in America.**
   False: According to Feeding America, 50 million Americans go to bed hungry and have no idea where their next meal will come from. Visits to food banks have risen 30 percent since the beginning of the recession.

6. **America takes care of its veterans.**
   Not true: The National Coalition for Homeless Veterans estimates that more than 67,000 veterans are homeless on any given night, but about 1.5 million are considered at risk of homelessness due to poverty, lack of support networks, or dismal living conditions and substandard housing.

7. **Government handouts created the nation's deficit.**
   False: The dominant factors that led to the deficit dilemma were Bush-era tax cuts, wars in Iraq and Afghanistan, the trade deficit, the mortgage crisis, and the Great Recession, not discretionary spending, which amounts to roughly 15 percent of the nation's budget.

8. **America's wealthiest pay more in taxes because they earn more.**
   It's "truthy" because it obscures the whole truth. The wealthiest wage earners pay about 21.5 percent

taxes on their personal income but not on capital-gains earnings. Until the 1990s, the capital-gains tax was 28 percent. Under Bush-era tax codes, the wealthiest Americans pay only 5.5 percent on capital-gain assets. According to the Obama administration, raising the capital-gains rate to 20 percent for those earning at least $250,000 a year would add another $12 billion to the treasury by 2014.

9. **Medicaid takes care of our seniors' health-care needs.**
   Not really. Medicaid and higher health-care expenditures have stretched elderly Americans' limited budgets beyond their means. Medical care spending for those between the ages of 55 and 64 is almost twice the amount spent by those between the ages of 35 and 44. Rising health-care costs are the major contributor to the rise in bankruptcy filings among the elderly.

10. **Poverty doesn't exist in the suburbs.**
    False. More and more people living in the nation's suburbs are losing their economic stability and landing in the ranks of the poor. The number of poor people living in the suburbs of metropolitan areas rose 24 percent—from 14.4 million in 2006 to 17.8 million in 2010. By comparison, the number of poor living in central cities rose by 20 percent.

FROM POVERTY TO PROSPERITY:
WHAT WILL IT TAKE?

> *"In a democracy the poor will have more power*
> *than the rich, because there are more of them,*
> *and the will of the majority is supreme."*
>
> —Aristotle

The end of poverty in America demands that we all change how we talk about, think about, feel about, and, more importantly, do something about it. Nothing will ever be done about poverty in America if we subscribe to Republican Rick Santorum's view about income inequality, "There always has been and, hopefully, . . . there always will be."

On the other hand, we will do nothing if we allow ourselves to be distracted and deluded by artificial signs of recovery, championed by too many Democrats. Both perspectives are predicated on an unhealthy economic divide in America. If the very foundation of our democracy teeters on a divide between the rich and the poor, we must either wake from our slumber or be prepared to face a uniquely American nightmare. If the very foundation of our democracy is based on a divide between the rich and the poor, and profits take precedence over people, the rich will live lavishly. But the rest of us and our economy will suffer.

What is our pain threshold? The numbers can't get much worse. Right now, one out of every two Americans is either in poverty or a razor-thin line away from being poor. This is our moment, and if we miss it, we fear it will be too late to stop a train speeding toward massive economic collapse. What will it take to move us from denying the poor to doing something about poverty?

This book was structured against the backdrop of history to remind us that we Americans have sacrificed and fought hard together for the common good throughout our history once we truly understood what we were sacrificing and fighting for. Our intention is to prod America's consciousness toward righteously radical thinking and 21st-century revolutionary action. With that said, we propose 12 policy-changing ideas that can help America move from an era of increasing poverty to a future of prosperity.

FROM POVERTY TO PROSPERITY: 12 POVERTY-CHANGING IDEAS

1. **Fundamental Fairness:**
   The rate of inflation has outpaced the rate of wage increases. Fundamental fairness means jobs with living-wage salaries and an economic system that lets people live above the poverty line so they no longer have to solely rely on welfare, food stamps, or other government subsidies for survival and upward mobility.

2. **Women and Children First!**
   We can't take care of America's 1.6 million impoverished children without creating living-wage job opportunities that allow single parents, especially mothers, to move out of poverty. We must invest in workplace day care and Head Start programs, so moms don't have to choose between earning a

living and caring for their children. Mothers must be able to work or secure job training while their children are cared for and educated. The value of Head Start programs that allow pre-school-age children to start school at a crucial learning time is well documented. What will it take for America to put her women and children first?

3. **The Jobs, Jobs, and More Jobs Plan:**
American manufacturing jobs are not coming back. So how do we face this extraordinary challenge? How do we overcome the dismal blue-collar job gap that leaves too many able-bodied workers unemployed? We can begin by instituting a 21st-century jobs plan built on providing our nation with services and products that are essential to our growth and survival. Many of our most low-skilled and unskilled citizens can be trained and immediately put to work on community-based infrastructure projects if we dare to match aptitudes to opportunities.

4. **Home Is Where the Heart Is:**
Homelessness is a national tragedy. The Great Recession and home foreclosures have left too many communities in shambles. America needs low-density public housing and a housing rehabilitation program to stabilize our communities and meet the most basic needs of our most vulnerable citizens. It's time to reassess properties and adjust mortgages based on true-market value and to end homelessness.

Americans who've lost homes due to foreclosure have stood up to authorities and started reclaiming abandoned properties. Bravo! Let's legitimize and legalize ways to cut through the red tape by developing a grassroots strategy that halts neighborhood decline and places people in vacant homes.

5. **Universal Food Delivery System:**
No one, especially children, should go hungry in America. We need a food delivery system that ends hunger and food insecurity; promotes small regional farms; supports urban farming initiatives; and offers new employment opportunities through the growth, harvesting, and distribution of food. If we do this one right, America can demonstrate its ability to tackle and solve complex human problems.

6. **Prisons & Mass Incarceration:**
Mass incarceration of minorities bankrupts the country; creates permanent, second-class citizenship; and locks formerly incarcerated individuals into on-the-street, economic concentration camps. Potentially salvageable people have been victims of the 20-year, race-based "War on Drugs" and a *criminal* criminal justice system. It's time for a major overhaul of the prison industrial complex.

7. **Privatization Versus Public Investment:**
The trend toward privatization of once publicly staffed and funded community enterprises means that, soon, all hospitals, schools, and prisons will be operated under the control of profit-driven

corporations. We must aggressively pursue public financing of education, the prison industrial complex, and health care. We call for transparency on all transfers of major public assets to private investors.

8. **The Fundamental Fairness Lobby:**
    We must no longer allow think tanks and lobbyists bankrolled by "haves" to summarily determine the fate of the "have-nots" and drive our nation's socio-economic policy. There are more than 13,000 lobbyists in Washington, many of whom champion the concerns of the wealthy. The poor need comparable representation that will advocate for fundamental fairness and challenge democracy-destroying schemes like Citizen's United, a Supreme Court decision that allows the wealthy to secretly buy elections.

9. **Equitable Progressive Tax Codes:**
    It's time to end tax breaks and concessions for rich corporations that outsource American jobs and hide profits in secret offshore accounts. Close the loopholes and let the rich pay their fair share of taxes.

10. **Recession Restitution Act:**
    In America, criminals are supposed to pay for their crimes. If you do the crime, you do the time. Those who fueled the Great Recession through deceit and malfeasance should be held accountable. Guilty parties must be required to pay restitution. Further, the government should institute an

immediate debt-forgiveness and reconciliation program for victims of proven predatory lending practices perpetrated on consumers during the recession and prohibit all endeavors to profit from poverty.

11. **Health Care Assurance:**
Nearly 45,000 people die each year because they lack health insurance. The uninsured are more likely to go without needed health care or depend on emergency rooms for primary care—often when treatable illnesses have progressed to untreatable stages. Despite the partisan debate and efforts to roll back health-care-reform efforts, all Americans must have access to quality health care and medical insurance with an available single-payer option.

12. **White House Conference on the Eradication of Poverty:**
If we are serious about ending poverty, there is no better way to set the national tone for our efforts than a White House Conference on the Eradication of Poverty in America. This undertaking, led by our President, will summon the best and the brightest from diverse viewpoints to seriously explore how we can end poverty—now. Those who participate will signal to the nation and the world that America is serious about establishing fundamental fairness in our society.

Many of these ideas may seem far too radical for our current socio-political environment. We offer them as an appetizer for all who hunger for radical, systemic change. That hunger will be nourished with knowledge as we explore these ideas further.

FUNDAMENTAL FAIRNESS

Poverty has melted the divide between the middle class, the working poor, and the persistent poor. Revised Census Bureau data show that there are 51 million people with incomes less than 50 percent above the poverty line. Of that number, about half (49 percent) are suburban whites. Black Americans comprise 18 percent and Latinos 26 percent.

Based on new Census Bureau methods that examined regional living costs (which vary from city to city), there were three other factors that pushed people into the lower-income bracket: taxes (more than 8 million); medical expenses (6 million); and work expenses (4 million), such as supplies, clothing, transportation, and child care.[85]

Let's do the math: Incomes that haven't kept pace with inflation + loss of manufacturing and outsourced customer service jobs + insufficient living-wage job creation + a recession that increased unemployment and downsized the middle class = the working poor.

THE MIDDLE CLASS DOESN'T LIVE HERE ANYMORE

Most economists agree that the typical middle class salary is about $35,000. A family with combined incomes of about $50,000 a year makes them "middle class." If that family earned $60,000 to $80,000, it is considered "solid" middle class. However, when we closely examine what it really takes to be middle class, we see a foundation that's far from solid. Any shift in the income equation can quickly plunge a family into low-income status.

For most American families, it takes two incomes to even meet the "middle class" benchmark. CareerBuilder, America's largest employment website, reported that eight-in-ten (77 percent) of American workers stated that they live paycheck to paycheck to make ends meet. One in five started missing bill payments in 2009, and 23 percent said they started living paycheck to paycheck that same year.[86]

This means that most middle class Americans are now only one grave illness, one serious accident, one termination, or one lost salary away from joining the low-income ranks. And this doesn't even take into account the ever-rising cost of living that eats up even more of Americans' weekly pay. Incomes have increased by only 20 percent within the past two decades, yet the cost of living has risen steadily. In May 2001, the average cost of a gallon of regular gas was about $1.70. While writing this book, the national average price for a gallon of regular gas in February 2012 was around $3.50. The cost of America's health insurance has also skyrocketed. In 2002, American families paid $979.1 billion in health care. Today, reports the *Health Affairs* journal, the cost is almost $2 trillion.[87]

So, if it takes two low-income salaries to qualify as "middle class" and that status is threatened every day by the cost of living, we have to question if being middle class is really more of an American aspiration than a reality.

A generation ago, families could get by with one well-employed breadwinner. Today, if we want to maintain the American middle class dream, two incomes are required, and any financial hiccup can upend that fragile middle class lifestyle. A generation ago, a backup earner could step into the workforce if the primary worker became disabled or unemployed. Today, both breadwinners are primary earners and equally essential to sustaining a family's livelihood.

Harvard University law professor and author Elizabeth Warren defined the "middle class" as "a state of mind"—what people *do* rather than what they actually earn or even hope to earn:

"Middle class people are people who mow the lawn, who pick up litter on the streets. They go to PTA meetings and invest not just in themselves, but in their children and communities," commented Warren in the ABC News series, *The Comeback: Defining the American Middle Class in Recession.*[88]

For families living one income away from complete economic collapse, a system of fundamental fairness is sorely needed to keep the poor and the working poor out of poverty and to stabilize what's left of the at-risk middle class.

A frank exploration of fundamental fairness in America will change the dialogue and policies aimed at the poor. It will prevent further erosion of the middle class, raise wages in line with the increased standard of living, and rebuild safety nets so that 150 million Americans can survive these extremely difficult times.

WOMEN AND CHILDREN FIRST!

If, as the popular song goes, "the children are our future," we're destined for a scary future. Poverty is cyclical. Odds are, a poor child today will wind up being a poor adult. According to Urban Institute, poverty repetition is substantially high for both Black and white children. The Institute's 2010 study, "Childhood Poverty Persistence: Facts and Consequences," says that among white children who are poor at birth, roughly a third (31 percent) will be persistently poor. More than two-thirds (69 percent) of Black children born poor will remain poor. With 1.6 million children living in poverty today, the need for immediate action is evident.[89]

U.S. Census figures show that there are more than 15 million families headed by women with no father in the house.[90] We can't take care of America's impoverished children without creating living-wage job opportunities that allow single parents, especially mothers, to move out of poverty. Research has already shown that the earlier a child starts school, the more likely he or she is to succeed academically. Therefore, if we are to address generational poverty, women and children must be our priority. Invest in workplace day care and Head Start programs, so moms don't have to choose between making a living and caring for their children. Mothers must be able to work or secure job training while their children are cared for and educated.

21ST-CENTURY MANUFACTURING

The United States has lost a staggering average of 50,000 manufacturing jobs *every month* since 2001. The country now ranks last among the top 15 manufacturing nations in terms of exported industrial production: an ominous portrait indeed. America's industrial decline has become so severe that Richard McCormack, Director of the National Intelligence Agency, reported in *Forbes* that he has started the process to assess the security implications of America's diminishing manufacturing activity.[91]

As William Julius Wilson of Harvard University has noted, America's manufacturing decline has been in motion for years, but has accelerated in the years leading up to the recession.

"The job loss among blue-collar workers has been about proportional to what we experienced of the Great Depression of the early 1930s," said Professor Andrew Sum, Director of the Center for Labor Market Studies at Northeastern University in Boston.[92]

Almost seven out of every ten jobs lost through the end of 2011 were construction, truck driving, warehouse, and other blue-collar jobs. The magnitude of those declines is "unprecedented," Sum said.[93]

A 21st-century jobs plan must unclog neighborhood-based economic engines. A good place to start firing up local economies is to expand models pioneered and proposed by numerous social business and micro-enterprise agencies. It is essential that we find innovative and unique ways to re-train the under-employed and unemployed with new skills for the new economy.

THE JOBS, JOBS, AND MORE JOBS PLAN

How do we face the extraordinary challenge of replacing manufacturing jobs? Again, the answer can be found in our proudest historic moments. When Europe was in economic shambles, we created the Marshall Plan to end famine and help the country rebuild. We need a similar effort today aimed at communities devastated before and because of the recession. In the previous chapter, "Poverty of Imagination," we discussed innovative ways to create environmentally friendly and cost-effective living spaces. Well, with a little vision, we can make those grand ideas a grand reality. We can help close the dismal blue-collar job gap and put able-bodied, low-skill and no-skill Americans to work on community-based infrastructure projects. If we dare match vision with needs, we can create dignified work that provides services and products that are essential for growth, survival, and better living. With a Marshall-type plan specifically aimed at struggling neighborhoods and grasping emerging opportunities, and with good living-wage paying jobs, we can shore up families battered by bills and rebuild our troubled nation.

THE PROFIT IN POVERTY

The new poverty numbers are forcing middle class families to rely on services that traditionally impoverished Americans have depended on for years.

According to the U.S. Department of Agriculture's February 2012 figures, over 46 million Americans (14

percent of the population) are now living on food
stamps with the average recipient receiving $150 worth
per month.⁹⁴ Actually, "food stamps" have had a make-
over in America. During the late 1990s, the government
phased out the facsimile printed money for a specialized
swipe-as-you-go debit-card system that can be processed
for purchases in grocery stores and major retailers just
like any other consumer.

For most of us, 46 million people poor enough
to qualify for food-stamp debit cards is a depressing
thought. But for banking and investment giant, JPMorgan Chase, every time a new welfare debit card is issued,
profits tick up a notch. The company is the largest, first,
and only contracted processor of food-stamp benefit
cards in America. In 2009, two years after the recession
officially began, the company posted profits of $11.7
billion on revenues of $115.6 billion—a 109 percent
jump and a 14 percent increase over the previous year.⁹⁵
Christopher Paton, manager with JPMorgan's public-sec-
tor benefit payments division, described how the welfare
card division contributed to company profits:

> "Right now, volumes have gone through the roof
> in the past couple of years. The good news, from
> JPMorgan's perspective, is the infrastructure that
> we built has been able to cope with that increase
> in volume."⁹⁶

Of course, from Paton's perspective, the company is
providing a social benefit, especially for the "new poor"
grappling with the stigma of poverty. National chains
such as Target, Costco, Wal-Mart, and Family Dollar are

also adjusting marketing and operational strategies to service the growing poor. Food-stamp debit cards are a convenience, especially for those unaccustomed to poverty.

Convenient or not, it's a bitter irony when multi-billion-dollar banking and investment companies make millions more off the poor millions who are making less. And JPMorgan Chase isn't the only banking institution showing robust growth in the shadow of the financial crisis. At the end of 2007, according to Reuters, JPMorgan Chase and three other institutions—Wells Fargo, Citigroup, and Bank of America—held 39 percent, or $3.8 trillion, worth of deposits. To give that some perspective, on that same day, June 30, 2007, the FDIC's Deposit Insurance Fund had a balance of only $10.4 billion.[97]

The same four institutions are also part of the $26 billion settlement agreement between the federal government and the nation's largest banks over allegations of widespread mortgage fraud.

Banks aren't the only institutions enjoying the bounty of the Great Recession. In 2009, when almost 3 million people lost their private health insurance, America's health insurance companies increased profits by 56 percent. According to a Health Care for America Now (HCAN) report, the nation's five largest for-profit insurers closed 2009 with a combined profit of $12.2 billion.[98]

Meanwhile, as more and more Americans are figuring out how to feed families on $150 a month, the mega-rich have gone back to spending on luxury items. *USA TODAY* declared in early 2011 that wealthy Americans have apparently decided it's "okay to splurge again."[99] The market is zinging again with purchases like $80,000 battery-powered bicycles; $525,000 timepieces; $630,000 sports cars; $1 million yachts; and vacation homes in posh locales such as Cape Cod, Massachusetts, and Hilton Head, South Carolina.

RECESSION RESTITUTION

Perhaps it's naïve to imagine that companies would invest profits in ways that would create good jobs for struggling Americans. Filmmaker Michael Moore, who addressed this issue during the "Remaking America" symposium observed:

> "Corporate America, the Fortune 500, are sitting on $2 trillion of cash in their bank accounts. In the past, that has never happened. What corporations do when they make money is they then spend a good chunk of that money to create more jobs. They say, 'Oh, wow; this thing we invented is doing really well. Let's build another factory, and we can make more of that and we'll employ more people.' That's how it used to kind of work.

> "Now what they're doing is making record profits and then putting the money in their bank account. They're doing it in part because it's their rainy-day fund. They know the other shoe hasn't dropped. They know the crash of '08 wasn't the last crash. They're still doing credit default swaps

and derivatives and all this crazy casino stuff on Wall Street. They know another crash could happen. They want to make sure that they're protected on their Noah's Ark where they've put their $2 trillion of cash."

Americans shouldn't be allowed to suffer while the rich celebrate their blunders with $500,000 watches and multimillion-dollar yachts. There must be justice. Through greed, deceit, and malfeasance Wall Street bankers helped plunge the country into recession and brought sheer misery into the lives of millions of American homeowners and workers. Because our government considered them "too important to fail" bankers were given more money that many used to pay themselves unprecedented bonuses. Every court in the United States has the statutory authority to order offenders to monetarily compensate the victims of their crime. Since it's highly unlikely that the super-rich, Wall Street bankers will ever be charged in a court of law, they must face the scrutiny and repercussions of the people's court. We need a federal Recession Restitution Act that demands compensation from the white collar criminals who victimized America.

HOME IS WHERE THE HEART IS

"Everyone has the right to a standard of living adequate for the health and well-being of himself and of his family, including food, clothing, housing, and medical care and necessary social services, and the

right to security in the event of unemployment, sickness, disability, widowhood, old age, or other lack of livelihood in circumstances beyond his control."

—The Universal Declaration of Human Rights

People living on the streets are exposed to human rights violations that include lack of sanitary conditions, exposure to disease, lack of shelter from the elements, robbery, rape, murder, unjust incarceration, and other horrors. Amnesty International cites the conflicting dynamics of 3.5 million homeless people in America while every day, "banks foreclose on more than 10,000 mortgages and order evictions of those residing in foreclosed homes."

We believe that adequate housing or some sort of safe shelter should be afforded to every citizen. In America, a country afflicted with a poverty of vision but a glut of available land and abandoned and foreclosed properties, solutions to housing and homelessness shouldn't be so far from our reach. A Universal Housing Plan will seek innovative and sustainable methods to create housing for everyone.

The Great Recession and home foreclosures have left too many communities in shambles. America needs low-density public housing and a housing rehabilitation program to stabilize our communities and meet the most basic needs of our most vulnerable citizens. Inspired by some of the survival techniques and bold actions of the homeless to reclaim and utilize foreclosed and abandoned homes, this plan will seek ways to turn some of those endeavors into viable housing options for the poor.

The Universal Housing Plan will strive to end the decline of neighborhoods and homelessness by legitimizing and legalizing efforts to reclaim foreclosed and abandoned properties. Pre-recession properties will be reassessed and mortgage payments reset at existing home values. This new approach to building sustainable communities—particularly those in disproportionately impacted communities of color—will also address the housing needs of qualified low-income homeowners.

UNIVERSAL FOOD DELIVERY SYSTEM

Visits to food banks are up 30 percent nationwide, according to Vicki B. Escarra, President and CEO of Feeding America. There are more than 50 million Americans in this country who are hungry and who have no idea where their next meal will come from. That number, she speculated during "Remaking America," represents the "new poor"—middle class Americans unexpectedly shoved into the ranks of the poor due to the recession. But widespread hunger was a problem long before the recession.

Although everyone agrees that children and the elderly, especially, should not go hungry—unprecedented numbers do. Even in boom and average economies, America has never solved the problem of hunger within its borders. We know that poverty, homelessness, hunger, and bad health—particularly in low-income communities with no access to fresh food—are all intertwined. This is why the poverty manifesto calls for the development of a universal food delivery system that not only addresses hunger in America, but also creates sustainable jobs in farming, processing, and transportation to local and national distribution centers.

Majora Carter, a pioneer in environmental equality and another panelist at "Remaking America," has long championed efforts to grow food in ways that will reach inner cities and rural areas, using emerging technologies that will bolster regional food systems. But she's not alone. Agencies such as The Food Trust, Will Allen's Growing Power, and PolicyLink have worked to pass legislation and develop models aimed at improving access to healthy, affordable foods and to educate children and families about nutrition.

Hunger in America is a problem with a solution. Of all the challenges this country faces—rich with fertile farm land and potential growing spaces in metropolitan areas—a new food delivery system should be the easiest to solve. A Universal Food Delivery System would support and work to expedite all local, national, and international efforts aimed at delivering fresh, canned, and packaged produce to the hungry and, in the process, create sustainable, living-wage jobs for Americans currently underemployed or unemployed.

PRISONS AND MASS INCARCERATION

There's another injustice against the poor seems to be growing in America. A November 2011 *Wall Street Journal* report confirmed that debtor prisons are making a comeback.[100] Borrowers who can't or don't pay their debts are now being sent to jail. Credit card companies have become very efficient at having arrest warrants issued for debts if the accused doesn't show up in court. Many people who are consumed with debt and trying to survive have missed court dates and wound up behind bars. In some cases, the article notes, the courts are turning some of the bail money over to credit card companies. Nationwide figures aren't known yet because most courts don't keep records of warrants by specific offenses. What is known, based on the *WSJ* article, is that more than one-third of states in this country have issued some 5,000 such warrants since the start of 2010.

This is just another justification for a complete overhaul of the prison industrial complex. There is a direct link between poverty and prisons that has disproportionally filled the nation's prisons with poor African Americans and Latinos. Remember, poverty isn't bound by race. What happened to the "old poor" now threatens the "new poor." Racial injustice aside, we should be outraged at a costly and corrupt system that sends a bankrupt poor person to jail for debt while morally bankrupt bankers go free after putting an entire nation in debt. It's time to put real "justice" in the criminal justice system.

PRIVATIZATION VERSUS PUBLIC INVESTMENT

There's a third tier in the poverty/prison matrix – profits. Altogether, states pay billions to house prisoners and private companies want their share. This probably explains why Corrections Corporation of America, the nation's largest for-profit prison operator, recently offered to buy prisons in 48 states. *The Huffington Post* obtained a copy of the letter sent to state officials and in February 2012 published an in-depth article about the proposed deal. According to the letter, Corrections Corporation of America's management offer came with an interesting caveat; a 20-year contract and an assurance that the prisons would remain "at least 90 percent full."[101]

This proposed prison deal speaks to a larger, more pervasive trend of our times—rich corporations' desire to privatize public institutions for profit. With cities and states suffering budget woes, privatization of public schools—via the charter school movement—hospitals, and mental health institutions is a welcomed option. We're not saying that private ownership or privatizing services to public institutions are across-the-board evil, we're saying that the profit motive of privatization can lead to dangerous outcomes. These institutions serve or house the poor; and, as the recession has taught us, profits outweigh the concerns of the people. We must reverse the trend. Public financing of public services must remain a priority.

FUNDAMENTAL FAIRNESS LOBBY

"The unemployed are politically invisible.
They don't make major campaign donations.
They don't lobby Congress.
There's no National Association
of Unemployed People."
—Robert Reich

There are more than 13,000 paid lobbyists in Washington, DC, serving as advocates for special interest groups and individuals. A publicly funded Fundamental Fairness Lobbying firm will advocate for legislation that improves the lives of the newly poor, the working poor, and the chronically poor. The Fundamental Fairness Lobby will attempt to defeat any institutional actions (criminal justice, banking, housing, health insurance, etc.) and legislation that jeopardize the well-being of its constituents, including discriminatory practices against the poor, housing and employment discrimination, and all predatory endeavors of the rich and powerful to profit off of poverty.

This effort will also create a means to legally address the denial of access to employment and social services, and make any other acts of discrimination against the poor unconstitutional and prosecutable under the law.

EQUITY TAX JUSTICE PLAN

There can be no fundamental fairness without equitable taxation of all citizens. Equitable tax legislation is essential to true economic recovery. Income Equity lobbyists will support passage of fair taxation legislation such as the "Buffett Rule," which will force the wealthiest 1 percent of Americans and major corporations to pay their fair share of taxes.

Income Equity lobbyists will pursue legislative agendas and review all tax code proposals. Fundamental Fairness lawyers will pursue new taxation ideas and support other plans and efforts, including the lowering of tax payments for low-income families and the working poor; taxation that boosts America's safety-net services and an increase of taxes on the rich; regulation and taxation of "paper" headquarters located in faraway lands that enable the wealthy to legally dodge their tax burdens; and the closing of tax loopholes and tax breaks that benefit corporations that outsource American jobs.

HEALTH ASSURANCE

According to a 2009 study conducted by Harvard Medical School and Cambridge Health Alliance, nearly 45,000 people die each year because they lack health insurance. Uninsured, working-age Americans, according to the researchers, have a 40 percent higher risk of death than their privately insured counterparts, up from a 25 percent rate found in 1993.[102] The uninsured are more likely to go without needed health care or wind up going to emergency rooms, often after preventable illnesses have reached advanced or deadly stages.

We recognize that the President's health care reform bill will make health care more available to millions of Americans in 2014, but we are also cognizant of the aggressive efforts, particularly from the Right, to overturn the bill. Regardless of partisan political machinations, no American should die because they lack health insurance or access to quality health care. Medical insurance with the single-payer option should become a reality for all Americans, and we must invest in publicly funded community health centers and hospitals. Then the poor and uninsured will have other options than emergency rooms as their only source for primary care or early death.

WHITE HOUSE CONFERENCE ON THE ERADICATION OF POVERTY

In order to bring all these ideas to fruition and add legislative muscle to a serious movement to help struggling Americans end poverty forever, we're calling for a White House Conference on the Eradication of Poverty.

On January 29, 2009, nine days after his inauguration, President Barack Obama signed the *Lilly Ledbetter Fair Pay Act*. In 1997, Lilly Ledbetter, a production supervisor at the Goodyear Tire plant in Alabama, filed an equal-pay lawsuit six months before her early retirement. In 2007, the U.S. Supreme Court ruled against Ledbetter *(Ledbetter v. Goodyear Tire & Rubber Co.)* with a decision that severely limited workers' rights under anti-discrimination laws. The *Lilly Ledbetter Act* restored the protections against pay discrimination.

Since 1909, the Executive Office of the President of the United States has sponsored national conferences to bring together the best minds in the nation to address critical national issues. The White House Conference on Civil Rights in 1966 and the ongoing White House Conference on Aging are but two of the more widely known policy think tanks convened under a President's initiative. White House Conferences convene the best of the best in the field of chosen interest to consistently meet, under a specified amount of time, with the goal of preparing a report for the President of the United States.

Each final conference report serves as the President's blueprint to call for executive and legislative action.

Convening the conference need not be a protracted affair. International and national programs and initiatives aimed at reducing and ultimately eliminating poverty already exist. The next President need only choose informed and committed citizens who will use their knowledge and skills to cull the best of the best from existing models and initiatives. Among them should be individuals who've coped with and found ways to overcome extreme poverty. Experts who serve as contributors and advisers should be intimately involved with the poor and keenly aware of their experiences and the challenges that they face.

THE THREE P'S: PRIORITY, PLAN, AND PATH

It should be obvious that we are neither politicians nor policymakers. We are democratic intellectuals blessed with public platforms to address issues that matter; and we are deeply committed to doing our small part to help bring about this conference.

In light of the millions now in poverty, combined with the unreal reality of a "jobless recovery," we're calling on everyday people from coast to coast to flood city, state, and federal government officials with a petition for the first official act of the next President on January 21, 2013, to be the announcement of a White House Conference on the Eradication of Poverty in America.

Tell the President to Convene a White House Conference on the Eradication of Poverty

Dear Mr. President:

I'm sick and tired of a country that only works for the 1 percent of the wealthiest Americans while millions of Americans face unemployment, underemployment, and poverty. I urge you to stand up for the struggling 99 percent and call for a White House Conference on the Eradication of Poverty that will lead to long-term solutions and living-wage jobs for all Americans.

Our country is in a state of emergency and in need of bold decisive leadership. Americans need jobs and immediate solutions to support the unprecedented number of citizens who are now trapped in poverty.

I believe this country has the resources and expertise necessary to end poverty, but this effort must become a national priority mandated by the highest office in the land.

In order to set legislative priorities that will end poverty once and for all, and to bring relief to millions of unemployed people and impoverished families, I'm asking that your first official act as President of the United States be the convening of a White House Conference on the Eradication of Poverty in America.

Sincerely,

[Your name here]

Now is the time for each of us to take personal responsibility in changing the dialogue about poverty. In this digital age, with YouTube, Facebook, Twitter, and other social-media tools, everyday Americans—who have lived through the Great Recession and lost their

middle class or working class footholds—have the opportunity to share their stories and their solutions with
those charged with solving the economic challenges
that they face. If the issue of poverty is articulated as
"fundamental fairness" we can create a mass movement
and add another proud chapter to America's legacy of
social transformation.

In preparation for the White House Conference, we
would hold ten Town Hall meetings around the nation
to allow the 99 percent from all walks of life to discuss
the reality of income inequality; stagnant wages; and
increased costs for food, housing, health care, and
education.

We recognize that the end of poverty can only be
addressed in a meaningful way if it is put squarely in the
context of America's new post-manufacturing economy.
We recognize that the challenges American citizens face
must be addressed simultaneously from the top down
and the bottom up. Without a commitment to consistent, people-powered pressure, we have little hope
that our representatives at every level of city, state, and
federal governments will lobby to make the conference
a national priority.

With 50 million Americans under siege, we must
move from the asylum of denial into the stadium of
game-changing action. Our children, our children's children, our country, and indeed the very future of democracy in America depend on how we respond to this very
real crisis.

When entire neighborhoods, cities, and states have
been brought to ruin, it is time to redefine and more

effectively fight poverty in America. When programs designed to stanch the bleeding of America's arteries have been bargained away to protect the interests of a fortunate few, the few must be challenged.

Unlike the wealthiest 1 percent, the perennially poor, newly poor, and near poor have no formidable champion or legion of lobbyists to defend their cause in Washington. When individuals can no longer turn to the shelter of extended family members or friends for aid and comfort—because everybody's been laid off—poverty takes on new meaning. The magnitude of the Great Recession confirms that poverty is no longer a personal calamity; it's a societal crisis.

Just as our nation was forced to diffuse the destructive language, negative stereotypes, and ingrained biases that allowed discrimination and oppression of Black people, handicapped people, gay and lesbian people, and others; we must now recalibrate the poverty climate in America. Destigmatization of poverty and the acknowledgement of its existence is the first essential step toward genuine eradication.

With a surplus of opportunity, affirmation, compassion, courage and imagination, we can make poverty an archaic remnant of how America used to be. Here's to those precious and priceless Americans on whose behalf this battle will be waged—and won!

The Poverty Tour:
A Call to Conscience

August 6 - 11, 2011
A Retrospective

"We wanted people who are struggling in this current economy to know that they are not alone and not forgotten."

—Tavis Smiley

"We want to speak truths about the suffering of everyday people, so that poor and working folks are empowered by the legacy of Brother Martin."

—Cornel West

On August 6, 2011, we boarded a bus and set out on our 18-city, 11 state Poverty Tour. It was an intense but enlightening journey. Our motivation was to call the nation's conscience to the plight of the poor in America. We heard tragic stories of struggle and strife and met people of all races challenged by the Great Recession. Yet, we were also inspired by acts of extraordinary resilience, determination and compassion. What follows is a day-by-day schedule of a tour that will remain in our hearts forever.

August 6, 2012
Hayward, Wisconsin
Our first stop was the Waadookodaading Ojibwe Language Immersion Charter School and the Lac Courte Oreilles Tribal Offices

in Hayward, part of a larger indigenous language preservation movement. The Wisconsin Reservation is making progress on the education fronts but still struggles with health and housing issues as their community emerges from poverty.

Au Claire, Wisconsin

In Au Claire, Wisconsin where local farmers have sold fruits, vegetables, and farm produce in the city for more than one hundred years. There we met farmers from the Hmong community; Vietnamese immigrants who came to the U.S. after the Vietnam War. We wanted to hear the story of immigrants who, in many cases, are facing even more challenges surviving in a country that's economically strained.

Madison, Wisconsin

Our bus pulled up just as a national activist group, "Take Back the Land-Madison" was protesting in front of a foreclosed duplex. The group that believes "housing is a human right" occupies foreclosed properties.

Later that evening, we sat with students and directors from the University of Wisconsin Madison's "Odyssey Project," an initiative that helps low-income people get into college. Meeting with clients who had benefitted from the project made our visit even more meaningful.

August 7, 2012
Milwaukee, Wisconsin

The first stop of Day Two of The Poverty Tour was Growing Power Farm and Facilities in Milwaukee. Half of the workers involved with this exciting project live in poverty. Growing Power's goal to empower community members so they can develop their own food systems and gain a sense of independence is indeed noteworthy.

Chicago, Illinois

We drove on to Chicago that day and stopped at the Martin Luther King Legacy Apartments, a 45-unit building that includes

housing for low-income families. The stop was a symbolic re-
minder of our mission because in 1966, Dr. Martin Luther King,
Jr. and his family—in an attempt to bring attention to the housing crisis facing African Americans—lived at the complex.

Joliet, Illinois

We made an essential excursion to Joliet, to speak with members
of Warehouse Workers for Justice—an organization founded by
the United Electrical Workers. This organization advocates tire-
lessly for its members. Warehouse and logistics workers shared
shocking stories of their battle for worker's rights in an environment where labor is undervalued and workers are underpaid.

Chicago, Illinois

When we returned to the familiar precincts of Chicago, it was
pouring rain. We gathered at St. Sabina's on the Southside for an
electrifying Town Hall Meeting. Hundreds of Chicagoans met us
for a rousing gathering with our host, the visionary activist pas-
tor Father Michael Pfleger. The St. Sabina community is engaged
in proactive efforts to ensure that their seniors avoid the downward economic spiral and abandonment that too often accompanies aging. Many of St. Sabina's seniors have been blessed to
live in the 80-unit housing complex that the church has built. It
embodies the African-American tradition of respect, honor, and
care for our elders.

August 8, 2012
Ann Arbor, Michigan

We parked our bus on the parking lot of an abandoned shopping mall and trekked along the shoulder of I-94 Freeway. Off
the beaten path, we were lead to "Camp Take Notice," a tent
city of middle aged white men and a few women who have lost
their jobs and their stature. This is the place that many poor and
homeless people now call "home."

Detroit, Michigan

Next, we headed to Detroit. Our first stop was Woodward
Academy where we spent time with the faculty and engaged

with schoolchildren whom 90% are eligible for free and reduced lunches. After leaving Woodward, we headed for a memorable Town Hall meeting at Detroit's City Hall. Rep. John Conyers (D-MI) was the featured speaker but the honest and pained voices of people struggling in this recession economy were the highlight of the event.

Akron, Ohio
We wrapped up the evening with a stop at the Miller Avenue United Church, in the poorest neighborhood in Akron. There we heard heartbreaking stories from military veterans who spoke of life on the streets and how poverty had ravaged the lives that they had once known.

August 9, 2012
Charleston, West Virginia
In Charleston, we were struck silent by the accounts of the survivors of the 2010 Upper Big Branch mine disaster that took the lives of more than two dozen miners. There, the topic wasn't as much about poverty as it was about rebuilding lives and communities after disaster strikes.

Capitol Heights, Maryland
Our trip to the Prince Georges' House Emergency Shelter—a site run by Catholic Charities and dedicated to single men, including military vets and the homeless was canceled due to compliance issues.

Instead, we slept on the cold hard streets of Washington, D.C. that night; at 3rd and E Street. Homeless teens, including a pregnant girl, kept us company as we sat on cartons and talked about life without a home underneath the stars.

August 10, 2012
Washington, D.C.
We checked in at the Progressive National Baptist Convention to help honor the legendary 93-year old Rev. Gardner C. Taylor, the 'poet laureate of American Protestantism.' Then we headed

to the DC Central Kitchen where formerly unemployed and/ or homeless cooks prepare meals that eventually makes it to shelters, transitional houses, and rehabilitation centers. DCCK's motto is to use food "as a tool to strengthen bodies, empower minds, and build communities."

August 11, 2012
Atlanta, Georgia

In the basement of the Old Ebenezer Church, we met members of the Georgia Association of Latino Elected Officials and documented and undocumented workers from Mexico. Just a half block away, we sat down with the founder of Truly Living Well Farm and discussed the farm's mission to develop a community-based food system in the heart of Atlanta.

Of course, our visit to Atlanta would not have been complete without paying respects to our hero and inspiration, Dr. Martin Luther King, Jr. We visited the tomb of Dr. King and his wife, Coretta Scott King, laid a wreath and gave praise.

Caledonia, Mississippi

We drove on to Caledonia, MI to the home of David and Lee Wilson. David, a military man, extended his stay in the Air Force so that his children could have medical benefits. The Wilsons opened the doors to their brand new Habitat for Humanity home and graciously allowed us to spend the night with their 10 kids, one dog and two cats.

Birmingham, Alabama

In Birmingham, we learned the power of personal and collective redemption during our visit with the Dannon Project. The organization works with people who were previously incarcerated for non-violent crimes. Again, we witnessed compassion in action through an agency that offers mostly young people a second chance and assists them in getting their lives back on track.

Columbus, Mississippi

That evening, we visited Wilma Minor. Her son, Stevie had his neck broken during a Magnolia Bowl football game. Stevie is a quadriplegic and for 16 years Wilma cared for him in a cramped, unsuitable home. We visited Wilma in her spacious new home built by Habitat for Humanity.

We stopped for a discussion with the Prairie Opportunity, Inc., a community action organization that fights poverty on the local level by providing services for low-income, elderly, and disabled families that promote self-sufficiency. The clientele we met seemed skilled, willing, able, and anxious to work. As far as they were concerned, the only missing component was available local jobs.

August 12, 2012
Clarksdale, Mississippi

In Clarksdale, we had a lyrical, musical, bluesy good time at the Ground Zero Blues Club where Coahoma Opportunities, Inc. and other local community service organizations teamed up to provide a free lunch for low-income families in a relaxing, empowering atmosphere.

Memphis, Tennessee

"The Poverty Tour: A Call to Conscience" appropriately ended in Memphis. First, we stopped at the National Civil Rights Museum where we met with some of the 1968 sanitation workers, the very people that Dr. King was fighting for before his assassination. We also met with current sanitation workers involved in a dispute with the city over a sanitation privatization plan that threatens their salaries and livelihood.

We concluded our sojourn with a visit to the site of Dr. King's death—the historic Lorraine Motel. The Poverty Tour came to its official end with another engaging town hall meeting at the Saint Andrew African Methodist Episcopal in Memphis Tennessee.

Notes

1   Byron Pitts, "Half of U.S. poor or low-income," Census Bureau data, CBS News, December 15, 2011, retrieved from http://www.cbsnews.com/8301-201_162-573343397/census-data-half-of-u.s.-poor-or-low-income/.

2   Annalyn Censky, "How the middle class became the underclass," CNN Money, February 16, 2011, retrieved from http"//money.cnn.com/2011/02/16/news/economy/middle_class

3   Don Peck, "Can the Middle Class Be Saved?," The Atlantic, September 2011, retrieved from http://www.theatlantic.com/magazine/archive/2011/09 /can-the-middle-class-be-saved/8600/?single_page=true.

4   Jesse Washington, "Food stamp families to critics: Walk in our shoes," January 26, 2012, retrieved from http://.www.equalvoiceforfamilies.org/2012/food-stamp-families-to-critics-walk-in-our-shoes/; and "Gingrich: Obama Is 'The Best Food Stamp President' in American History," CBS News, January 19, 2012. CBS News reported that "Gingrich has made a habit of calling President Obama the 'food stamp president'—a nickname he . . . has often painted [as] the contrast between himself and Mr. Obama as a choice between paychecks and food stamps," retrieved from http://mediamatters.org/research/201201190015.

5   Ibid.

6   Judy Mosca, "Poorhouses in 19th-Century America," helium.com, created July 19, 2009, retrieved from http://www.helium.com/items/1521990-poverty-in-america/.

7   Michael B. Katz and Mark J. Stern, "Poverty in Twentieth-Century America," America at the Millennium Project, Working Paper #7, November 2001, retrieved from http://www.sp2.upenn.edu/america2000/wp7all.pdf

8   Jerry D. Marx, Ph.D., "Women, Settlements, and the Redefinition of Poverty," The Social Welfare History Project, date unknown, retrieved from http://www.socialwelfarehistory.com/eras/women-settlements-and-poverty/.

9   Ibid.

10 "Rosie the Riveter: Women Working During World War II," The National Park Service's online exhibit of artifacts, photos, and stories of the American World War II Home Front, retrieved from http://www.nps.gov/pwro/collection/website/home.htm/.

11 Katz and Stern, "Poverty in Twentieth-Century America."

12 Ibid.

13 Michael Harrington, *The Other America: Poverty in the United States* (New York: Macmillan Books, 1962).

14 Maurice Isserman, "Michael Harrington: Warrior on Poverty," *The New York Times,* June 19, 2009; retrieved from http://www.nytimes.com/2009/06/21/books/review/Isserman-t.html?_|=1.

15 Katz and Stern, "Poverty in Twentieth-Century America."

16 James Truslow Adams, *The Epic of America* (New York: Little Brown & Company, 1931 First Edition).

17 Woodrow Wilson, First Inaugural Address, March 4, 1913, retrieved from www.bartleby.com/124/pres44.html/.

18 David Kamp, "Rethinking the American Dream," *Vanity Fair,* April 2009, retrieved from www.vanityfair.com/culture/features/200904/american-dream200904/.

19 Ibid.

20 For more information, visit http://www.metlife.com/individual/life-advice/personal-finance/american-dream-study/index.html.

21 Marisol Bello, "Report: Child homelessness up 33% in 3 years, USA TODAY, December 13, 2011, retrieved from http://www.usatoday.com/news/nation/story/2011-12/homeless-children-increase/51851146/1; and National Coalition for the Homeless, September 2009, retrieved from http://www.nationalhomeless.org/factsheets/veterans.html/.

22 "Poverty in America: A Threat to the Common Good," Catholic charities Policy Paper, 2006; retrieved from http://www.catholiccharitiesusa.org/documentt.doc?id=2920

23 Kathryn Edin on research in South Philadelphia; interviewed by Don Peck for "How a New Jobless Era Will Transform America" / March 2010 / The Atlantic.com / Retrieved from: http://www.theatlantic.com/magazine/archive/2010/03/how-a-new-jobless-era-will-transform-america/7919/

24 Julia Cass, "'Held Captive': Child Poverty in America," Children's Defense Fund, Washington, DC, December 20, 2010, retrieved from www.childrensdefense.org/child-research-data-publications/data/held-captive-child-poverty.html/.

25 Julia Cass interview with Robert Jamison, founder and director of the North Delta Youth Development Center, Lambert, Mississippi, 2009.

26 The National Center on Family Homelessness, "America's Youngest Outcasts 2010," December 2011, retrieved from http://www.homelesschildrenamerica.org/whatsnew.php.

27 Children's Defense Fund, *State of America's Children,* 2011 (Washington, DC: Children's Defense Fund, 2011), retrieved from www.childrens-defense.org; and Patrick McCarthy, Executive Director of the Annie E. Casey Foundation, interview on *Tavis Smiley* on PBS, August 23, 2011, retrieved from http://video.pbs.org/video/2102593097#.

28 Marian Wright Edelman "Children Can't Vote but You Can – And Must"Child Watch® Column /October 22, 2010 http://www.childrens-defense.org/newsroom/child-watch-columns/child-watch-documents/children-cant-vote-but-you-can-and-must.html

29 Michael Harrington, *The Other America.*

30 Richard Nixon, addressing the presidential nomination at the Republican National Convention, Miami Beach, Florida, August 8, 1968.

31 Francis Wilkinson, "Benign Neglect," *The New York Times,* June 11, 2008, retrieved from http://campaignstops.blogs.nytimes.com/2008/06/11/be-nignneglect; and Adam Clymer, "Former Senator Daniel Patrick Moyni-han Dead at 76," *The New York Times,* March 26, 2003, retrieved from http://www.nytimes.com/2003/03/26/obituaries/26CND-MOYNIHAN.html?ex=10948752008&en=382d07780ef51612&ei=5070/.

32 President Carter delivered his "Crisis of Confidence" televised speech on July 15, 1979; retrieved from http://www.pbs.org/wgbh/americanexperience/features/primary-resources/carter-crisis/.

33 Jeffrey Sachs was interviewed October 13, 2011, in "Nothing Moves without Us," part 4 of the Poverty Tour, on the *Tavis Smiley* show on PBS, transcript retrieved from http://video.pbs.org/video/2153490649/.

34 Peter Dreier, "Reagan's Legacy: Homelessness in America," The National Housing Institute, Issue #135, May/June 2004, retrieved from http://www.nhi.org/online/issues/135/reagan.html/.

35 Ibid.

36 Robert Lekachman, *Greed Is Not Enough: Reaganomics* (New York: Random House, 1982).

37 Kristin Seefeldt et al., "At Risk: America's Poor During and After the Great Recession, White Paper, School of Public and Environmental Affairs, Indiana University –Bloomington, January 2012.

38 Distinguished author Barbara Ehrenreich spoke to present-day attitudes regarding the poor at the "Remaking America: From Poverty to Prosperity" symposium held January 12, 2012, at George Washington University in Washington, DC, and nationally televised on C-SPAN.

39 Peter Dreier, "Reagan's Real Legacy," *The Nation,* February 4, 2011, retrieved from http://www.thenation.com/article/158321/reagan-real-legacy. President Reagan defends himself against charges of callousness, retrieved from reaganyears.tripod.com/reaganquotes.htm.

40 Ibid.

41 Ehrenreich, "Remaking America" symposium.

42 Ibid.

43 "The *Smiley & West* Poverty Tour Stops at ABC, C-SPAN, and MSNBC," Rush Limbaugh Show, August 11, 2011, transcript retrieved from http://www.povertytour.smileyandwest.com/2011/08/1846. "The *Smiley & West* Poverty Tour Stops at ABC, C-SPAN, and MSNBC," *Rush Limbaugh Show,* August 11, 2011, transcript retrieved from http://www.povertytour.smileyandwest.com/2011/08/1846.

44 *United States Department of Agriculture:* Personal Responsibility and Work Opportunity Reconciliation Act (P.L. 104-193, 110 Stat. 2105) Aug. 22, 1996 / Retrieved from: http://www.fns.usda.gov/snap/rules/Legislation/history/PL_104-193.htm

45 Sanford F. Schram and Joe Soss, "Success Stories: Welfare Reform, Policy Discourse, and the Politics of Research," *The Annals of the American Academy of Political and Social Science,* Vol. 577, September 2001, retrieved from http://www.jstor.org/pss/1049822.

46 Liz Schott and LaDonna Pavetti, "Many States Cutting TANF Benefits Harshly Despite Unemployment and Unprecedented Need," Center on Budget and Policy Priorities, October 3, 2011, retrieved from http://www.cbpp.org/cms/?fa=view&id=3498.

47 Visit the Website for each candidate—current or former—for a variety of quotable perspectives..

48 Robert Rector and Rachel Sheffield, "What Is Poverty in the United States Today?," The Heritage Foundation, July 19, 2011; retrieved from http://www.heritage.org/research/reports/2011/07/what-is-poverty.

49 "Official USDA Food Plans: Cost of Food at Home at Four Levels, U.S. Average," U.S. Department of Agriculture, Center for Nutrition and Policy Promotion, July 2011, retrieved from http://www.cnpp.usda.gov/Publications/FoodPlans/2011/CostofFoodJul2011.pdf/.

50 Bruce Watson, "Does It Really Cost This Tea Party Congressman $200,000 to Feed His Family?", retrieved from http://www.dailyfinance.com/2011/0919/does-it-really-cist-this-tea-party-congressman-200-000-to-feed/.

51 On the July 26, 2011, edition of *The Colbert Report,* Peter Edelman explained why America cannot call the troops home and beat its plowshares back into swords when it comes to fighting the War on Poverty; retrieved from http://www.colbertnation.com/the-colbert-report-videos/393169/july-26-2011/poor-in-america-peter-edelman.

52 Ilyce Glink, "Tea Party: Don't Let Renters Vote," CBS News, December 1, 2020, retrieved from http://www.cbsnews.com/8301-5055145_162-37143350/tea-party-dont-let-renters-vote/.

53 Tonya Weathersbee, "Tea Party Just Rich Whites Exploiting Poor Ones," blackamericaweb.com, October 6, 2010, retrieved from http://www.blackamericaweb.com/?=articles/news/baw_commentary_news/22569/.

54 Matt Taibbi, "The Truth about the Tea Party: Matt Tiabbi takes down the far-right monster and the corporate insiders who created it," Rolling Stone.com, September 28, 2010, retrieved from http://www.rollingstone.com/politics/news/matt-taibbi-on-the-tea-party-20100928/.

55 "Many See Those In 'Poverty' As Not So Poor," Rasmussen Reports.com, August 19, 2011, retrieved from http://www.rasmussenreports.com/public_content/lifestyle/august_2011/many_see_those_in_poverty_as_not_so_poor/.

56　Lymari Morales, "Fewer Americans See U.S. Divided Into 'Haves,' 'Have-Nots,'" Gallup.com, December 15, 2011, retrieved from http://www.gallup.com/poll/151556/Fewer-Americans-Divided-Haves-Nots.aspx/.

57　"45% Say Government Programs Increase Poverty in America," Rasmussen Report, April 6, 2011, retrieved from http://www.rasmussenreports.com/public_content/business/general_businesss/april_2011/45_say_government_programs_increase_poverty_in_america/.

58　"Bill O'Reilly, Tavis Smiley, and Cornel West Have Fiery Clash Over Wall Street, Poverty" (video), *Roland Martin Reports*, October 12, 2011, retrieved from http://rolandmartinreports.com/blog/2011/10/bill-oreilly-tavis-smiley-and-cornel-west-have-fiery-clash-over-wall-street-poverty-video/.

59　Bruce Watson, "It's Official: Weath Gap Has Turned America Into a Seething Pit of Class Resentment," Daily Finance.com/January 13, 2012, retrieved from http:// www.dailyfinance.com/2012/01/13/its-official-wealth-gap-has-turned-america-into-a-seething-pit/.

60　Howard Zinn, *A People's History of the United States: 1492–Present* (New York: Harper Perennial, 2003).

61　The Industrial Revolution, History.com, retrieved from http://www.history.com/topics/industrial-revolution, and http://www.history.com/topics/child-labor/.

62　Andrew Gavin Marshall, *Robber Barons, Revolution, and Social Control: The Century of Social Engineering, Part I,* Global Research.ca, March 10, 2011, retrieved from http://globalresearch.ca/index.php?context=va&aid=23639/.

63　See "The Industrial Revolution: child labor, retrieved from http://www.history.com/topics/child-labor/.

64　S. Mintz, "Learn about the Gilded Age," 2007, retrieved from http://www.digitalhistory.uh.edu/.

65　Stephanie Siek, "King's Final Message: Poverty is a civil rights battle," CNN, January 16, 2012; retrieved from inamerica.blogs.cnn.com/tag/Stephanie-siek-cnn/

66　"Beyond Vietnam / A Time to Break Silence" full transcript retrieved from Martin Luther King, Jr. Online: http://www.mlkonline.net/vietnam.html

67　Teresa Tritch, "How the Deficit Got This Big," *The New York Times,* July 23, 2011, retrieved from http://www.nytimes.com/2011/07/24/opinion/sunday/24sun4.html.

68　David Szydloski, "'The Costs of War': A Must-Read Study, published by the Watson Center for International Studies at Brown University, September 23, 2011, retrieved from http://inthesetimes.com/ittlist/entry/12001/the_costs_of_war_a_must_read_study/.

69　Ibid.

70　Bill Lyne, "Fortunate Sons and Daughters," United Faculty of Washington State Blog, November 12, 2009, retrieved from http://www.ufws.org/content/fortunate-sons-and-daughters/.

71   John Glaser, "Billions Lost in Secret Federal Reserve Funding of Iraq War," retrieved from http://news.antiwar.com.2011/10/25/billions-lost-in-secret-federal-reserve-funding-of-iraq-war/.

72   "State of Homelessness in America," National Alliance to End Homelessness, retrieved from www.endhomelessness .org/content/article/detail/3668; and Ellem Bassuk, M.D. et al., "America's Youngest Outcasts 2010," National Center on Family Homelessness 2010 Report, retrieved from http://www.homelesschildrenamerica.org/media/NCFH_AmericaOutcast2010_web.pdf/.

73   Stephanie Siek, "King's Final Message."

74   "Facing the School Dropout Dilemma," The American Psychological Association, retrieved from http://www.apa.org/pi/families/resources/school-dropout-prevention.aspx/.

75   Julia Cass, "'Held Captive," Children's Defense Fund.

76   Roger Caldwell, "Single parents more likely to be below poverty line, according to Census," Imperfect Parent, September 17, 2011, retrieved from http://www.imperfectparent.com/topics/2011/09/17/single-parentsspmore-likely-to-be-below-poverty-line-according-to-Census/.

77   Les Christie, "Number of people without health insurance climbs," *CNNMoney*, retrieved from http://money.cnn.com/2011/09/13/news/economy/census_bureau_health_insurance/index.htm

78   Bruce Western and Becky Pettit, "Incarceration & Social Inequality," The American Academy of Arts & Sciences, Summer 2010, vol. 139, no.3.

79   Alexander, *The New Jim Crow.*

80   Peter S. Goodman, "Despite Signs of Recovery, Chronic Joblessness Rises," The New York Times, February 20, 2010, retrieved from http://www.nytimes.com/2010/02/21/business/economy/21unemployed.html?scp=1&sq=despite%20signs%20of%20recovery,%20joblessness&st=cse

81   Charles Duhigg and Keith Bradsher. "'Jobs aren't coming back' to U.S.," *The New York Times,* January 23, 2012, retrieved from http://www.herald-tribune.com/article/20120123/ARTICLE/301239999?p=1&tc=pg/.

82   Anika Ananda and Gus Lubin, "Iconic Products That America Doesn't Make Anymore," Businessinsider.com, November 1, 2010, retrieved from http://www.businessinsider.com/19-iconic-products-that-america-doesnt-make-anymore-2010-11#ixzz1mBKEsDG7/.

83   For more information about the programs and plans that helped salvage Europe after World War II, visit (1) the Truman Plan, U.S. National Archives and Records Administration, http://www.archives.gov/exhibits/featured_documents/marshallplan; (2) the Marshall Plan, Spartacus.schoolnet.com, http://www.spartacus.schoolnet.co.uk/USAmarshallP.htm/; and (3) What economic conditions existed in Europe after World War II? Answered by Discovery channel, http://curiosity.discovery.com/question/european-economic-conditions-after-wwii/.

84   Jeffrey Sachs on *Tavis Smiley,* details at endnote 33

85   Jason DeParle, Robert Gebeloff, and Sabrina Tavernise, "Older Suburban and Struggling, 'Near Poor' Startle the Census," *The New York Times*, November 18, 2011, retrieved from http://www.nytimes.com/2011/11/19/us/census-measures-those-not-quite-in-poverty-but-struggling.html?emc=eta1/.

86   "Number of Workers Living Paycheck to Paycheck at Pre-Recession Levels, Reveals New CareerBuilder Survey, CareerBuilder Press Release, August 11, 2011, retrieved from http://www.careerbuilder.com/share/aboutus/pressreleasedetail.aspx?id=pr651&sd=8/111/2011&ed=8/11/2099/

87   Judy Isikow, "The Comeback: Defining the American Middle Class Recession," *ABC World News Special Report,* "Ten years ago, health insurance cost American families $979.1 billion per year. Today, America is spending $1.88 trillion . . . according to *Health Affairs,* a leading journal of health policy in the United States," retrieved from http://abcnews.go.com/WN/comeback-diane-sawyer-reports-american-middle-class/story?id=10085746/.

88   Ibid.

89   Caroline Ratcliffe and Signe-Mary McKernan, "Childhood Poverty Persistence: Facts and Consequences," Brief 14, The Urban Institute, June 2010, retrieved from http://www.urban.org/uploadedpdf/412126-child-poverty-persistence.pdf/.

90   Households and Families: 2010 Census Summary File, retrieved from http://factfinder2.census.gov/tables/services/jsf/pages/productview.xhtml?pid=DEC_10_SFL_QTP11&prodType=table

91   Lorenn Thompson (contributor), "Intelligence Community Fears U.S. Manufacturing Decline," 2/14/2011, Forbes.com, retrieved from http://www.forbes.com/sites/beltway/2011/02/14/intelligence-community-fears-u-s-manufacturing -decline/

92   Molly Line, "Job Hunt: Blue Collar Workers Struggle Most," Fox News: Live Shot Blog, March 23, 2010, retrieved from http://liveshots.blogs.foxnews.com/2010/03/23/job-hunt-blue-collar-workers-struggle-most/#ixzz1nd5eEPu6/.

93   Ibid.

94   "Supplemental Nutrition Assistance Program: Number of persons participating," U.S. Department of Agriculture, data as of February 1, 2012, retrieved from http://www.fns.usda.gov/pd/29SNAPcurrPP.htm/

95   Kimberly Weisul (contributor), "23 who laughed at the recession," *CNNMoney.com,* April 28, 2010, retrieved from http://money.cnn.com/galleries/2010/fortune/1004/gallery.fortune500_recession_big_profits.fortune/index.html/.

96   Margaret Brennan, Host, Interview with JP Morgan 's Paton, Discusses U.S. Food Stamp Use, interview with Christopher Paton, Bloomberg.com video, January 8, 2012, retrieved from http://www.bloomberg.com/news/2010-10-08/jpmorgan-s-paton-says-food-stamps-use-to-keep-rising-video.html/

97   Rolfe Winkler, "Break Up the Big Banks," Reuters, September 15, 2009, retrieved from HTTP://BLOGS.REUTERS.COM/ROLFE-WIN-KLER/2009/09/15/BREAK-UP-THE-BIG-BANKS/

98   Emily Walker, MedPage Today Staff Writer, "Health Insurers Post Record Profits," February 12, 2010, retrieved from http://abcnews.go.com/Health/HealthCare/health-insurers-post-record-profits/story?id=9818699#.TOJ1iPQiiCs.email/

99   Gary Strauss, "For the wealthy, a return to luxury spending," *USA TODAY,* February 21, 2011, retrieved from http://www.usatoday.com/money/economy/2011-02-21-1Aluxury21_CV_N.htm#

100   Jessica Silver-Greenberg, "Welcome to Debtors' Prison, 2011 Edition," *Wall Street Journal,* March 17, 2011, retrieved from http://online.wsj.com/article/SB10001424052748704396500457620455381163660.html/.

101   Chris Kirkham, "Private Prison Corporation Offers Cash in Exchange for State Prisons," Huffington Post.com, retrieved from http://www.huffingtonpost.com/2012/02/14/private-prisons-buying-state-prisons_n_1272143.html/.

102   David Cecere, "New study finds 45,000 deaths annually linked to lack of health coverage," reveals the Cambridge Health Alliance. Uninsured working-age Americans have 40 percent higher death risk than privately insured counterparts, September 17, 2009, retrieved from http://news.harvard.edu/gazette/story/2009/09/new-study-finds-45000-deaths-annually-linked-to-lack-of-health-coverage/.

Acknowledgments

Tavis Smiley and Cornel West wish to express our deep gratitude to Sylvester Brown, Jr., for his detailed empirical research and creative contribution to this work.

We are especially grateful to Cheryl Woodruff for her editorial genius and substantial stewardship of this book.

We are deeply indebted to two magnificent executive assistants, Jessita Usher and Lili Pollock, whose patience and perseverance proved invaluable in the writing of the text.

Special thanks to Juan Roberts/Creative Lunacy, Cindy Shaw/CreativeDetails.net, Debi Rose Catalano, Paulette Robinson, Thomas Louie, Kirsten Melvey, and Nicolette Salamanca.

And finally, to the entire team at The Smiley Group, Inc., for their support of our work and witness to raise poverty higher on the American agenda via the various media and public platforms we are blessed to have.

About the Authors

From his celebrated conversations with world figures to his work to inspire the next generation of leaders as a broadcaster, author, advocate, and philanthropist, **Tavis Smiley** continues to be an outstanding voice for change. Currently, Smiley hosts the late-night television talk show *Tavis Smiley* on PBS; *The Tavis Smiley Show* distributed by Public Radio International (PRI); and is a co-host of Smiley & West (PRI). He is the first American to simultaneously host signature talk shows on both public television and public radio. In addition to his radio and television work, Smiley has authored 16 books, including his *New York Times* bestselling memoir *What I Know For Sure* and the book he edited, the #1 *New York Times* bestseller, *Covenant with Black America.* He is also the presenter and creative force behind America I AM: The African American Imprint—an unprecedented and award-winning traveling museum exhibition celebrating the extraordinary impact of African American contributions to our nation and to the world. In 2009, Tavis Smiley was named one of *TIME's* "100 Most Influential People in the World."

Educator and philosopher **Cornel West** is the Class of 1943 University Professor at Princeton University. Known as one of America's most gifted, provocative, and important democratic intellectuals, he is the author of the contemporary classic *Race Matters,* which changed the course of America's dialogue on race and justice; the *New York Times* bestseller *Democracy Matters;* and the memoir *Brother West: Living and Loving Out Loud.* He is the author of 17 other texts and the recipient of the American Book Award. West holds more than 20 honorary degrees, and will return this fall as Professor of Philosophy and Christian Practice at Union Theological Seminary in New York City.